BANG!

BANG!

Getting Your Message Heard
in a Noisy World

LINDA KAPLAN THALER AND ROBIN KOVAL

WITH DELIA MARSHALL

Currency   Doubleday

NEW YORK   LONDON   TORONTO   SYDNEY   AUCKLAND

A CURRENCY BOOK
PUBLISHED BY DOUBLEDAY
a division of Random House, Inc.

CURRENCY is a trademark of Random House, Inc., and DOUBLEDAY is a
registered trademark of Random House, Inc.

Book design by Platinum Design, Inc.

Library of Congress Cataloging-in-Publication Data
Kaplan Thaler, Linda.
Bang! : getting your message heard in a noisy world / Linda Kaplan Thaler and
Robin Koval, with Delia Marshall.—1st ed.
p.   cm.
Includes index.
ISBN 0-385-50816-6
1. Advertising. 2. Marketing. 3. Attention-seeking. I. Koval, Robin.
II. Marshall, Delia. III. Title.
HF5823.K265   2003
659.1'13—dc21
2003051502

Page 8, photo courtesy of BBDO New York; page 10, Getty Images; page 24, © 2002 American Family Life Assurance Company
(AFLAC); page 26, 2002 NYTimes Co.; page 27, People Weekly © 2002 Time, Inc., all rights reserved; page 35, photo courtesy
of Wendy's International; page 39, © 1998 The American Red Cross; page 48, © 2001 Pilot Pen Corporation of America; page
54, © 2003 DCI Studios; page 61, © 1996 Heineken USA; page 85, © 2000 Parmalat USA/© 2000 Irv. Blitz; page 96, © 2002
Blimpie International, Inc., page 99, © 2003 Reckitt Benckiser, Inc.; page 129, © 1996 Geoffrey, Inc.; page 131, © 2000 Continental Airlines; page 134, Young Clinton H3-02, July 1963 Rose Garden, White House Credit: Consolidated News Photos; page
139, © 1985 Eastman Kodak Company; page 148, © 2003 Verizon Wireless, used with permission; page 150, courtesy of the
Partnership for a Drug-free America®; page 158, © 2002 C. Elizabeth Watt; page 161, Mr. Potato Head® & © 2003 Hasbro, Inc.,
used with permission; page 191, © 2001 American Family Life Assurance Company (AFLAC); page 205, © Ruby Tuesday, Inc.,
2003, all rights reserved; page 210, © Callard & Bowser-Suchard, Inc., 2003; page 217, the Forevermark is used under license.

PRINTED IN THE UNITED STATES OF AMERICA

First Edition: November 2003

All trademarks are the property of their respective companies.

SPECIAL SALES
Currency Books are available at special discounts for bulk purchases for sales
promotions or premiums. Special editions, including personalized covers,
excerpts of existing books, and corporate imprints, can be created in large
quantities for special needs. For more information, write to Special Markets,
Currency Books, specialmarkets@randomhouse.com

3   5   7   9   10   8   6   4

To everyone at the Kaplan Thaler Group,
whose extraordinary talents are rivaled only by their
unbounding spirit and compassionate hearts.
—Linda & Robin

ACKNOWLEDGMENTS

To list everyone we want to thank in the writing of *Bang!* would be a book in itself. Because, in truth, it is the result of countless experiences, client partnerships, and years of collaborative working relationships. But we will attempt to thank at least some of the many people who have made this book possible.

First, thank you to Denise Larson, who came bounding into the office the summer of 2001, insisting that we put our creative philosophy into print. Denise, we hope the fruits of our labor have done justice to what you imagined that day.

Thanks to Richard Abate, our literary agent at ICM, the one who first saw our creative Big Bang thinking as the basis for a marketing book. He has never ceased to amaze us with his creativity, thoughtfulness, and passion for our work. None of this would have happened if you had not believed in us.

A special thanks to our talented and dedicated editor, Roger Scholl at Doubleday, and his assistant, Sarah Rainone, whose comments, additions, *and* subtractions made every page more readable, more fluid, more insightful. A kinder, gentler editor one could not hope for. And thank you to Meredith McGinnis, David Drake, and

Laura Pillar for their marketing help in promoting *Bang!* And we are very thankful to our book publicists Barbara Cave Henricks, Mark Fortier, and Lynn Goldberg at Goldberg McDuffie Communications for their expertise and advice. Thanks to the talented team at ElectricArtists, Marc Schiller, Howie Kleinberg, and Ethan Beard.

We want to thank the many clients, past and present, who have lent us their time, their stories, their never-ending passion for their businesses. We learn from you every day and are eternally thankful for the opportunity you have given us to bring Big Bang thinking to your brands and your consumers.

A very special thank you to Roy Bostock, former Chairman and CEO of the MacManus Group, who believed in the Kaplan Thaler Group enough to make us part of the MacManus/Bcom3 global network. We would not be writing this today without your faith in our potential success. And to Craig Brown, former President and COO of Bcom3 and Roger Haupt, President and COO of Publicis, now our parent company, who have been fans of our literary endeavor from the get-go. Also, a thank you to Maurice Lévy, CEO of the Publicis Groupe, for his support and inspirational quotes.

They say a book cannot be judged by its cover, but thanks to Rob Snyder's artistic eye, the exploding light bulb he conceived gives a powerful visual symbol of what's contained within the pages. Also, we'd like to thank Whitney Pillsbury, another brilliant art director at KTG, for the "out on a limb" photo he conceived for the back cover and his wonderful mock KTG "ad" in chapter 1. To Stuart Pittman and Nikki DeFeo, thanks for "brightening" the pages of *Bang!* with your wonderful art direction. Also, a special thanks to Joe Kelsey for shooting not only the back cover but our personal photos as well. And a thank you to Robin Schwarz for her humorous addition to the end of the book.

A generous thank you to Delia Marshall for all her help in cowriting *Bang!* with us. Your talent, humor, and positive energy made this collaboration one we shall never forget.

A heartfelt thanks to world-renowned bestselling author James

Patterson for his support of our book. You were a brilliant inspiration when you ran the J. Walter Thompson agency. And thanks to Burt Manning, former CEO of Thompson, whose advice has been a constant source of comfort and support for over twenty years.

Through the many months of working on this book, we are grateful to all the Kaplan Thaler folks who have given their time to help us realize this publication. Fran Marzano and Eneida DelValle, our assistants, for their dedication and late hours; Gerry Killeen, Managing Director of Creative Services, a never-ending fountain of support and constructive criticism; Lisa Bifulco, Head of Broadcast Production, who helped resolve countless talent issues related to the book; Ann Garreaud, our CFO, for her invaluable counsel as we ventured into this new arena; and Amy Frith who, with Paige Miller's assistance, worked tirelessly to buy and clear photos we so desperately needed. And, of course, thank you to graphic designer Alison Vicidomini, who put all the artwork together for this book.

A special thank-you to Tricia Kenney, who heads our public relations department, who went well above and beyond her role to help us finish *Bang!* From securing quotes, to checking references, to scheduling speaking engagements and interviews, Tricia is a true professional whose drive and determination ensured things were always done well. Additional thanks to Greg Davis and Dawn Terrazas, who, along with Tricia, have worked so hard to help make *Bang!* a success in the marketplace.

A special thank-you to Dr. Ona Robinson for her invaluable insights into the human psyche.

Thanks to our generous friends Evan Greenberg, Leslie Jacobus, and Joe Rella at Allscope Media for donating their time and insightful media expertise.

To our respective families, Fred, Michael and Emily Thaler, and Bertha and Marvin Kaplan, you are a constant source of comfort and joy, and to Kenny and Melissa Koval, your support has been unwavering from the beginning. Without the love of our families, it would have been a book without a heart.

Finally, we'd like to thank the gentleman who enabled the Kaplan Thaler Group to exist in the first place—Steve Sadove, the former president of Clairol and now Vice Chairman of Saks. Taking a chance on our small five-member start-up company took courage and faith, as well as a belief in our ability to create a Big Bang for your business.

We hope this book enables marketers everywhere to do the same.

If we've missed you, please accept our apology and fill in the blank. Our sincerest thanks to _____, without whom this book would not have been possible.

CONTENTS

WHAT IS A

BIG BANG,

ANYHOW?

These days, getting people to notice you isn't easy. The Information Age has morphed into Information Overload. Messages are everywhere: At the bottom of golf cups on the putting green, flashing on ATM screens, even posted over urinals (an excellent product placement for Budweiser). People gazing out the window when flying into O'Hare a few years ago couldn't escape the colossal rooftop sign advertising Altoids. Urban strivers can now turn to promotional high-rise video screens to avoid the ever-dreaded elevator eye contact. Come-ons decorate coffee cups, umbrellas, commuter train schedules, shopping carts, delivery trucks, lampposts. We even put an ad at the bottom of this page.

So how do you get heard? How does your company connect with the consumer?

You need a Big Bang.

When The Kaplan Thaler Group opened for business six years

ago, we knew that everything taught in Marketing 101 is no match for this daily deluge of data. We'd spent almost two decades creating campaigns that were tremendously successful, but we weren't exactly sure why. We knew that they were well liked, communicated with our consumer, got remembered—even entertained. But before we could go much further we needed to try to decipher the science behind our million-dollar ideas. We needed to understand what was unique about our way of thinking and working. We didn't want to feel that every time we approached a new campaign we had to reinvent the wheel.

Robin, who spends her spare time reading books that could top Mensa's advanced reading list, just happened to be boning up on cosmology at the time. "What about the big bang?" she suggested to me one day. "Isn't that the kind of work we do for our clients?" OK, so advertising isn't rocket science. It may seem like a pretty big leap from physics to promoting shampoo, but the more we thought about it, the more it seemed like the right analogy. After all, our best ideas often come from seemingly random events, we work in a pressure-cooker environment, and, once released, our work tends to expand exponentially in the culture. And so, unknown to the Nobel Foundation in Sweden, the KTG Big Bang Theory was discovered.

And it's worked. A Big Bang was responsible for nearly doubling the annual sales growth for AFLAC insurance company. A Big Bang took Herbal Essences from a nearly extinct shampoo to a $750 million worldwide brand. The Big Bang theory has catapulted The Kaplan Thaler Group from a small business in the top floor of a townhouse to the fastest-growing agency among the top 100 in the United States. Starting with just $27 million in billings in 1997, we now have a roster of blue-chip clients with over $450 million in billings.

So what, exactly, *is* a Big Bang in business? More to the point, how do you turn your company into a Big Bang factory? First, let's go back—*waaay* back.

In the beginning, say, 15 billion years ago, give or take a few days if you factor in leap years, there were no planets, stars, or galaxies. There was simply blank emptiness (think of the recent ABC fall line-up). One could interpret this state of nonbeing as a peaceful serenity, void of anything except, well, void. But nothing was further from the truth. In fact, this tabula rasa was seething with "all the pent-up energy of a primordial explosion," as the physicist Trinh Xuan Thuan put it in *The Birth of the Universe: The Big Bang and After*. But you probably couldn't see all this seething because it was happening in a teeny, tiny space about $\frac{1}{3,000}$th of an inch in diameter (a size difficult to visualize unless you have ever rented a studio apartment in Manhattan). And it was really, really, hot, 10^{32} degrees Kelvin, which would make even tankinis unwearable.

Then, suddenly, a cosmic clock struck and the whole universe exploded onto the scene, hurling out electric particles, photons, and other matter every which way. When matter was created, it was neutralized by anti-matter, but luckily there was more matter than anti-matter, or we'd all be the opposite of who we are today.

But the universe didn't stop there. It just kept expanding and expanding and expanding. It spawned stars and planets and dark holes and eventually spit out billions and billions of other universes. And slowly certain chemical combos begat crude biological organisms, starting with the lowliest amoeba and working up to life-forms as complex as plumbers and used car salesmen. For those of you who cut high school physics to smoke Marlboros behind the tennis courts, this was the original Big Bang.

Well, a Big Bang in the marketplace is similar, minus a galaxy or two. The Real Thing. iMac. Just Do It. Gucci. Martha Stewart. *The Sopranos*. Starbucks. These are all Big Bangs. They all started out as an idea and rapidly went on to take over the cultural universe. In the early 1990s, for example, Gucci was a small manufacturer that had fallen out of favor with the fashionista crowd. Then they promoted a junior designer named Tom Ford. Now Gucci is a global synonym for fashion.

Our Big Bang theory has been so successful that we believe it is tailor-made for any company looking to increase market share exponentially.

Why does your business need a Big Bang? A Big Bang is designed to help make a brand explode onto the marketplace virtually overnight. In this world of shrinking timeframes and global competition, no one has the luxury of time to get the point across. Many clients are public companies, which means they live in a ninety-day world, under tremendous pressure to produce results before the next quarterly earnings statement. A Big Bang creates an ever-expanding universe for a product, and turns occasional users into fierce loyalists. A Big Bang cuts through the clutter and gets people to sit up and take notice. A Big Bang helps you to make the sale, close the deal, get the gig *now*. Here's why:

A BIG BANG DISRUPTS. At its core, a Big Bang idea is about taking the spotlight. It is about ideas that are simply too outrageous, too different, too polarizing to go unnoticed.

There is a sea of sameness out there. We're glutted with products and services. You can't go anywhere without seeing the same mind-numbing brands over and over again. Drive down the highway in California and you'll pass by a strip mall with Gap, Barnes & Noble, Old Navy, The Home Depot, Bed Bath & Beyond, and a gas station. Go through a couple of stoplights, and the whole thing starts all over again. Was that last fast-food joint a McDonald's or a Burger King? Who can tell the difference anymore?

On a recent trip to Hong Kong, Robin, never one to pass up a shopping opportunity, brought back—nothing. "Here I was in this exotic city halfway around the world," she told me when she returned. "I walked out my hotel room door, ready to load up on Far Eastern exotica, and all I saw were signs that said Gucci, Chanel, Escada. What's the point of lugging all that stuff back to New York?" Turns out that Hong Kong is just like New York, except that it has fewer Chinese restaurants.

A Big Bang bucks conventional wisdom and stops people in their tracks. According to *The Economist* magazine, people see over

3,000 messages each day, but like cooked spaghetti, only a couple of them stick to the wall. As a result, no one is sitting on the edge of his or her seat waiting to hear what you have to say. You need to disrupt the established paradigm to get through.

Let us give you an illustration of a recent campaign that was wildly successful, primarily because it was so unexpected. In the weeks following the World Trade Center attacks, when tourists were staying away from New York City in droves, Phil Dusenberry, former chairman of BBDO North America, and Ted Sann, chief creative officer of BBDO New York helped spearhead a campaign to convince people to come back to New York. "The BBDO team started with the idea that everybody has a New York dream," remembers Dusenberry. "So we wanted to say, 'Come find yours.' "

It took the BBDO team only a day or so to come up with an uplifting campaign, called "The New York Miracle," starring celebrities fulfilling their dreams: Woody Allen skating at Rockefeller Center ("You're not going to believe this," Allen breathlessly says after a series of spins and turns, "but that was the first time I was ever on ice skates!"). Henry Kissinger running the bases at Yankee Stadium ("Derek who?"). Barbara Walters auditioning on Broadway. Billy Crystal and Robert De Niro arguing about who gets to be the turkey and who gets to be the pilgrim in the Macy's Thanksgiving Day Parade.

"We knew we had a good idea," says Dusenberry, "but we didn't know that it would take off like a rocket." Moments after Mayor Giuliani aired the commercials for the press at Manhattan's City Hall, Dusenberry got a call from MSNBC's Brian Williams. Williams said, "If you come on my program tonight, I will play every one of these commercials completely, top to bottom." So Dusenberry went on the show. Most of the networks ended up donating time to run the spots. It played in countries all over the world, even as far away as Japan. Rudy Giuliani, in his book *Leadership,* attributes the campaign to restoring the spirit of New York, and getting people all over the world to come back.

The campaign was breakthrough because it starred celebrities who ordinarily refuse all requests to appear in a commercial. But just as important, the spots themselves grabbed the spotlight. At a time of national mourning and fear of the city, the spots relied on an unexpected bit of New York humor to take the spotlight.

A BIG BANG IS ILLOGICAL. Edward De Bono, the father of lateral thinking, noted that problem solving involves abandoning accepted, logical thought processes and rearranging and reevaluating the status quo. Often the reason we don't come up with better solutions to problems is simply because the existing ones seem to work just fine. "Why would I want a VCR when the movie theater is just around the corner?" might have been the response to the SONY engineer who designed the first home videocassette recorder. If we allow a little illogic into our thoughts, however, we can break through the prison of current convention. Somehow or other you have to embrace the idea that whatever business you are in, the most illogical course of action is often the most logical thing to do.

WOODY ALLEN HILARIOUSLY FULFILLING HIS ICE-DANCING FANTASY IN "THE NEW YORK MIRACLE" CAMPAIGN.

Plenty of American icons are perfectly ridiculous products if you think about them logically. Look at SUVs. Why would anyone want to drive vehicles that are too big for the garage, that guzzle gas, and that roll over when you turn too fast? It's totally illogical that white-collar city dwellers and soccer moms would want to drive "blue-collar" trucks. However, when you reorient your way of thinking from the "logic" of car as transportation to the "illogic" of car as fantasy, it's easy to understand that in a world where we often feel small and unnoticed, a big, 10,000-pound hunk of steel lets us feel important and impossible to overlook. SUVs are totally illogical, yet they are the most popular new car design in decades.

And who would have predicted the success of Starbucks? For years, all our caffeine cravings were fed by a fifty-cent visit to the local diner. Then along comes a place with concoctions such as "mocha malt frappuccino," and we can't stand in line long enough to blissfully shell out five bucks for it. And for that five bucks, you don't even get a waiter to give you a refill. Then they have the audacity to call their smallest cup of coffee a Tall, perhaps in the hopes that you won't notice how much you overpaid for it. But remarkably, Starbucks went from seventeen stores in 1987 to nearly 5,000 in 2002. No wonder they call it StarBUCKS.

Twenty-seven years ago, if you wrote a business plan on how to make money by selling water, you'd die of thirst waiting for the loan approval. For years and years people just turned on the tap and had a drink. For free. Then came Perrier. Some French genius thought, Hey, I'm going to fill a bottle with water and charge those Americans for it. And suddenly we were all convinced that expensive water made us better, healthier, smarter, more sophisticated. This is the most illogical thing you can think of! What's next, you ask? Well, in cities around the country, oxygen bars are now available to the discerning breather. Just what we need, more airheads.

Both Starbucks and Perrier used elegantly simple concepts—a cup of coffee and a glass of water—in a completely surprising way: to tap into our complex need to feel pampered and special. Scientist Stephan Wolfram, the author of *The Foundation for a New Kind*

IF YOU CAN SELL PEOPLE WATER, ANYTHING'S UP FOR GRABS.

of Science, notes, "Whenever a phenomenon is encountered that seems complex, it is taken for granted that it must be the result of an underlying mechanism that is itself complex. But my discovery is that simple programs can produce great complexity."

The beauty of Big Bang marketing ideas is that they don't require Deep Blue and a roomful of Ph.D.s. They just require the insight to realize that very few things are exactly what they seem. You must forget about what makes sense and open yourself up to the real reason why a particular brand or product is appealing. Illogical thinking means that when you're asked to promote a bottle of water, you realize that water is the last thing you should focus on. Great, explosive marketing or advertising ideas will only rise to the surface when everyone at the company is able to reject what worked in the past and embrace this kind of counterintuitive thinking.

A BIG BANG HAS A DRAMATIC, IMMEDIATE AND IRREVERSIBLE IMPACT. Big Bang marketing ideas disrupt because they are "discontinuously innovative." They reject the notion of incremental or evolutionary thinking and instead look for step-change solutions. They alter the landscape forever by introducing a way of thinking about a product or service that did not exist previously and that changes our entire pattern of behavior and attitudes about it.

It was exactly this kind of thinking that led to a brilliant marketing move by Mattel in the early 1980s. By this point, Barbie was a permanent resident of virtually every little girl's bedroom. This saturation naturally caused Mattel no end of grief as they realized their future sales would be dependent on mere clothes and accessories. Then Jill Barad, a lowly product manager at the time, came up with the discontinuous marketing concept that Barbie could be several different people at once. She could be a stylish executive, a dancer, or an ice skater, and little girls could have as many as their hearts (and their parents' wallets) desired. This brand-new way to market Barbie catapulted the creature from a $200 million product to a $1.9 billion brand.

FedEx is another great example of a discontinuous innovation. Before FedEx, you waited—and waited—for the mail to arrive. If it took five days for an important business document to arrive what could you do? It was simply "in the mail." FedEx completely changed this behavior. Magically (to the dismay of those of us who

11

called in sick to catch up on much neglected closet organization), the report prepared in Houston on Tuesday night now arrives in Cincinnati on Wednesday morning. (The Internet, of course, has raised the ante yet another level.)

Creating a discontinuous innovation requires that you stop thinking about the current situation and the momentary day-to-day problems and dream about the ideal situation. Ted Turner, a famous discontinuous innovator, was called crazy when he floated the notion of a twenty-four-hour news channel that would have correspondents all over the world. How could that possibly be done? Who could build such a network from scratch? It would cost millions and take forever. Furthermore, no one wants to watch news twenty-four hours a day, and frankly, there isn't that much news around. Ted considered those issues mere technicalities, and stuck to his dream. He focused on the end point (not the roadblocks on the way) and guess what? CNN is arguably the reason why the newspaper industry is scrambling for its life.

If a marketing campaign is to have the impact that CNN and FedEx had on our culture, then you must have the courage to come up with a whole new approach for the problem at hand.

Take Procter & Gamble's successful new Swiffer mop. True, the technology is terrific: Swiffer products don't simply swish dirt around, they actually attract dirt, making their disposable pads a veritable magnet for filth. But the marketing folks needed a disruptive idea to convince shoppers to toss their trusty brooms en masse. At first glance, a new kind of broom hardly seems like a must-buy. It was in a few focus groups, says Robert McDonald, president of global fabric and home care, that P&G finally found what it was after: Whenever people started to talk about their new Swiffer, they actually smiled. This led to the illogical marketing campaign that cleaning can be *fun*. P&G worked carefully on the design, says McDonald, ensuring "that it was cute, attractive, and appealing."

From this early research, P&G knew that once a consumer had

used a Swiffer, he or she would be hooked. So they swept the country with in-store demos and discount coupons—all based on the premise that "Swiffering" is a lot more fun to do than "cleaning." The marketing drive was hugely successful and now Swiffer products are responsible for $800 million in sales. With the Swiffer, P&G virtually invented a new category of products in the U.S.—called "Quick Clean"—and now, with their "Stop cleaning, start Swiffering," campaign, the concept has been expanded to wet mops and dusters.

A BIG BANG CAN'T BE IGNORED. Big Bang ideas are intense ideas. They are intentionally polarizing. You must have a point of view about them. They are the six-hundred-pound gorilla in the room. They must be dealt with. They force opinions. Yes, some folks think the AFLAC duck and his incessant quack is annoying. We are incredibly pleased about that. Yes, a few conservative organizations have criticized the sensual content of the Herbal Essences commercials. Our response? *Bring it on.*

If you have an idea that no one hates, everyone will forget it. Think about it. No one dislikes vanilla—but you can get that from anyone, anywhere. Talk to an ice cream connoisseur about his favorite flavor, however, and he might wax poetic about driving five miles out of his way to get a three-dollar cup of Ben & Jerry's Phish Food.

Big Bangs get noticed not just because they are unorthodox, however. They are also right for the moment. Timing is critical whenever you put a message, idea, service, or proposal out into the business marketplace. Howard Schultz, the chairman of Starbucks, knew that the time was ripe for putting a European-style café on every street corner. His great insight was to see that his product is not about coffee. It's about the experience. It's about having a gathering place. It's about small indulgences in a world that doesn't have time for big indulgences. It's about making a person feel rich because she can afford not only a $3.50 cup of coffee, but also the tip for the guy who doesn't clean up after her.

Here's another example of Big Bang timing. In 1968 Boeing lost a design competition for a large military jet contract. They decided not to waste all that work, tinkered with the design a bit, and turned it into a passenger plane. Most aviation experts at the time figured a big passenger jet was a waste of time: Everyone thought the supersonic age was around the corner, and that the Concorde would soon rule the skies, claims Clive Irving in *Wide-Body: The Triumph of the 747*. But Boeing bet on the fact that the masses were ready to fly immediately.

The 747 turned out to be the most successful aeronautical vehicle ever created. The world's first jumbo jet, the 747 revolutionized travel by enabling people to go long distances for a price they could afford. Its predecessor was the 707, Boeing's first passenger jet, which pioneered international jet travel, albeit at prices that were then beyond the means of many travelers. The 747 literally relegated the "jet set" to history. It's the reason any of us have ever had too many rum punches on a Caribbean beach.

A BIG BANG BECOMES AN ICON. There are a plethora of successful brands and products out there that are ubiquitously recognizable, and profitable to boot. But the ones that truly leapfrog their competitors have elevated themselves into an icon status. They have surpassed their pragmatic function and actually play a role in people's lives. These brands fulfill some human need or desire, which exponentially elevates their value in the marketplace.

When you drive a Lexus, for example, you're traveling in an excellently designed, well-appointed automobile. But get behind the wheel of a Mercedes-Benz, and you've already "arrived" before you've left the driveway. Owning a Mercedes is a symbol of one's financial success, one's elevated status in society, one's unqualified acceptance into the snootiest of country clubs. Buy your wife diamond earrings at Zales Jewelers for your twenty-fifth anniversary and she'll be tickled pink. But if you present those studs snugly ensconced in Tiffany's classic blue box instead, her eyes will sparkle with adoration, and you may never have to take the garbage out again. A Tiffany diamond is the symbol of one's eternal love, rivaled only by the passion its stock owners feel every time someone pays retail for its jewelry.

Easily one of the world's greatest icons today is Kodak, in large part because George Eastman had a pretty clear picture of how to make a Big Bang in the photography business. Although he never even completed high school, Eastman gave the world its first simple camera in 1888, registering it under the name Kodak. He devised the name himself, starting with the letter K because his mother's name was Kilbourn. He was an anagram fan, and, after trying out a number of letter combinations, he came up with Kodak. Combining this decisive-sounding word with yellow and red—considered one of the strongest and most vibrant color combinations—he instantly made the logo easy to recognize.

But it didn't take long for George Eastman to give his roll a much more profound role to play in our culture. His early camera was priced at $10, which was beyond the reach of ordinary folk. Then, in 1900, Kodak came out with the $1 Brownie, a cheap and simpler version of his original. Soon everyone in America was taking pictures. The Brownie was such a hit, in fact, that it provided Eastman with the opportunity to create the ultimate marketing Big Bang.

In 1930, on the thirtieth anniversary of the Brownie camera, posters across the country boasted: "Parents! Children! This camera free to any child born in 1918!" Five hundred thousand children who turned twelve that year were given a free Brownie camera by Kodak. This radical and risky marketing move ensured that following generations would become hooked on picture taking. Millions of families went on to preserve their most precious moments for decades to come. Kodak became America's storyteller, and has been saving the best "times of our life" for over 100 years.

A BIG BANG IS EVER EXPANDING. The earth keeps spinning and so does a Big Bang idea. Although it must remain centered on its core philosophical ideals, it has to be constantly remodeled and retuned to fit the eclectic rhythms of our rapidly changing world.

Back in 1989, the Energizer Bunny hopped onto the scene, wreaking havoc as he merrily marched through a series of "fake" commercials. With the core idea that the Energizer battery could outlast anyone, each ad started out looking like a typical commercial, only to be interrupted by a drum-banging bunny that just wouldn't stop. The Energizer Bunny became the quintessential symbol for longevity and endurance, and his popularity virtually topped any two-legged pop personalities of his era.

But his icon status as the ultimate go-getter didn't stop with the 115 spots he has starred in. For over a decade, the Energizer Bunny has been beating his drum at countless community events around the country, blew himself up to become the world's largest hot air balloon, and even plopped his little lucky rabbit's foot into cyberspace.

The Energizer Bunny was chosen as one of the top ten ad icons of the twentieth century by *Advertising Age,* because he is an ever-adapting symbol that keeps "going and going and going."

One of the most successful campaigns that KTG ever created had all of the ingredients mentioned above. It ruffled the feathers of the entire category because the ads were impossible to ignore. The campaign created an icon that represents all of us who feel like we're not getting heard. It was the quintessential Big Bang. Actually, it was more like . . .

The Big Quack

On an itchy, mosquito-infested vacation in the summer of 1999, I decided to take a break from scratching and check my voice mail. Buried in all of the messages was one from a woman with a southern accent. She said she was with AFLAC, an insurance company. AFLAC. AFLAC? Never heard of it. Probably some itty-bitty local company that needs help with a print ad or something, I thought to myself. I get a lot of these calls every week, and didn't think much of it. I quickly passed the call along to Robin, whose steel-trap memory can recall the gill size of a puffer fish. Robin listened to the southern woman's message and thought, "AFLAC. AFLAC? Never heard of it."

Usually advertising agencies get excited when clients come offering their business. In this case, however, no one at the company had ever heard of the client, which meant they probably had a budget that could fit into a piggy bank. And they were trying to sell *insurance*. Hardly the slam dunk we were looking for. Still, since KTG has a solid set of ethics, every call gets returned (we once had a telemarketer from Verizon who nearly went into shock when we politely rang *her* back). Robin called the southern woman back.

She found herself talking to Kathelen Spencer, the executive vice president and director of corporate relations for AFLAC, a company based in Columbus, Georgia. Spencer was genteel, poised, charming, perfectly polished. In her disarming southern way she told Robin that a mutual friend had recommended KTG as an agency that could get AFLAC some attention. Would we be interested in getting together for a chat?

In her significantly less beguiling New York accent, Robin tried to think of the most delicate way to find out what the hell AFLAC was.

Robin finally discovered that AFLAC sold some kind of supplementary insurance. Spencer said that AFLAC had been advertising for about ten years, yet she felt that it wasn't getting the awareness that it deserved (you could say *that* again, Robin thought). "We know that insurance is a difficult category, it isn't sexy, and people don't like to think about it," she elaborated. AFLAC was looking for a company like KTG—small, a little outrageous, highly creative—to put the company on the map.

Great. Another anonymous company with a tiny budget that wants us to magically transform its bottom line. Nevertheless, fledgling KTG was in no position to turn away business. Robin told Spencer that KTG would love to learn more about her company, and would certainly be willing to have a meeting with her team.

"Just one more thing," Robin asked. "What sort of advertising budget did you have in mind?"

In the world of advertising, anything less than $5 million is considered chump change. Robin suspected that this polite AFLAC lady wasn't ready to pony up more than $2 or $3 million—barely enough to pay for a pile of posters. Best to get the money issue on the table.

"Well," Spencer decorously responded. "Last year we spent $40 million."

Robin nearly dropped the phone. Two thoughts immediately ran through her mind: 1) Boy, do these people need a new advertising agency, and 2) I can't let her talk to another soul.

They made a date two weeks into the future, and Robin hung up. She immediately got the KTG troops to find out just who we were dealing with. AFLAC, we soon learned, is an extremely successful Fortune 500 company, traded heavily on the New York Stock Exchange. Employers around the country offer AFLAC insurance as an employee benefit, to fill gaps in traditional health insurance such as deductibles and loss of earning power. Basically, AFLAC insurance is for life-threatening injuries or catastrophic illnesses such as cancer. AFLAC is the largest provider of this supplementary insurance in the world.

When they contacted us, AFLAC had been working with the same agency for years. But the commercials were standard issue for an insurance company, tear-jerker vignettes as warm and mushy as a freshly baked Toll House cookie: "Why do you need this insurance? . . . Because he's got his mother's eyes." They were gentle, caring, emotional, focusing on beautiful children and families. But that's what every insurance company was doing, so they were blending into the woodwork. And AFLAC's $40 million—as huge a number as it is—was really a dwarf compared to the budgets of Allstate or MetLife.

Our two-week investigation revealed that AFLAC had spent in the neighborhood of $100 million on advertising during the previous years. *But no one had ever heard of them.* For an advertising agency with just one full year under its belt, this was a major opportunity.

So we shlepped down to Columbus, Georgia, to meet the AFLAC folks. We discovered that AFLAC is a family-founded business, run by Daniel Amos, the chairman and CEO, the son of one of the cofounders. Amos runs the whole operation with a few key decision makers. He's as friendly and disarming as can be, but beneath that down-home Georgia demeanor is a brilliant mind.

So what did Amos want his advertising to communicate? Well, unlike many clients, who demand that their thirty-second ads contain more information than the genetic map of a Mediterranean fruit fly, Dan Amos had only one request. He just wanted people to remember the name of his company. Ten years of advertising, and no one even knew who they were or what they did! Amos would travel across the country, he told us, and people could never seem to introduce him correctly.

Here was the deal: We were asked to come up with four potential spots. These spots would be tested against four created by their current ad agency. Whoever came up with the highest-scoring ad won.

I asked Amos if there was anything he didn't want to see in the ad campaign. Did he want to put any limits on our creativity? "No," he quickly replied. "I don't want to get involved in the creative process at all." I was astonished. In advertising, this is like a child saying he would prefer to skip Christmas and do extra-credit homework instead. It was especially surprising in light of the fact that this guy runs a company that sells cancer insurance—a delicate issue to say the least.

I needed to make sure that I'd heard him right. As the meeting was ending, I looked straight at Amos and carefully said, "Would you consider humor?" Amos leaned across the table, looked directly into my face, and replied, "I don't care if you have to show a naked man tap-dancing on the roof. I don't care *what* you do as long as you get people to know the name of this company."

I nodded my head and packed up, readily assuring him that we could create advertising that would make AFLAC a household name.

Truth is, aside from renaming the company Tide, we didn't have a clue how to make AFLAC a household name. And AFLAC being a forgetable acronym for the American Family Life Assurance Company (try saying *that* three times without spraining your tongue) made the task all the harder. But the folks at our place have a fervent belief in our collective talents. Each of us was confident that someone else would come up with a fabulous idea.

We had six weeks to complete the assignment. And then we had five weeks, and then four and then three and then two panic-stricken weeks until we needed to come up with a blockbuster. We had certainly been working. We had come up with sentimental commercials, celebrity endorsements, invented clever spokespeople, all sorts of stuff.

A few days before our deadline, Tom Amico and Eric David (one of our talented creative teams), convinced that we hadn't yet cracked the nut, were still working. "Every time we came up with an idea for a campaign—even a campaign we liked—we would say, 'But are you going to remember who it's for?'" remembers Tom. "We had all seen too many Super Bowl spots that were good, even great, except when it came to the part of remembering who they were for."

Eric went out to pick up some lunch and spent the next hour walking around the block saying the name over and over in his head. He got increasingly frustrated ("Why, of all names to get people to remember," he recalls thinking, "*AFLAC?*"). He started to say the word out loud. On Fortieth Street, right in front of a ten-dollar-dress store, as he said "AFLAC!" in an exasperated tone of voice, he realized that he sounded like a duck. He ran back to the office.

Tom, who had remained inside, suddenly looked up to find

Eric standing over his desk holding a bagged takeout order. Eric said, "AFLAC!" with a nasal affectation, imitating a quacking duck. As they looked at each other, "Our eyes got as wide as the cramped office that we were in," remembers Tom.

He turned around to his computer and they wrote the very first AFLAC duck spot over the next five minutes.

The commercial is entitled "Park Bench":

> *Two businessmen sitting on a park bench during lunch hour, tossing leftover bread crumbs to a flock of nearby ducks. A guy rides by on a bike, then you hear a resounding crash and see his bike upend in the distance.*
>
> *First businessman:* Boy, when I got hurt and missed work, I'm glad I had supplemental insurance.
>
> *Second:* Supplemental insurance? What's that?
>
> *One of the ducks:* AFLAC.
>
> *First guy:* Well, even the best insurance doesn't give you cash to cover things like lost pay and other expenses. This does.
>
> *Second:* What does?
>
> *Duck:* AFLAC!
>
> *First guy:* You should ask about it at work.
>
> *Second:* What's it called?
>
> *Duck: AFLAC!!!*
>
> *First pauses, then shrugs:* I don't know.
>
> *Second guy tosses a crumb to the duck. Duck groans, kicks the crumb back at the guy, and then shakes his head in frustration.*

The minute Eric and Tom showed me a rough mock-up of the ad, I got chills. This is usually a good omen.

But not everybody immediately saw the wisdom of a spokes-duck. I showed the ad to Robin and Gerry Killeen, our managing director of creative services. They were both aghast.

Gerry turned to me and said, "You wouldn't seriously bring this to the client, would you?"

"Well, I think America will remember the name," I replied.

"You've got to be kidding!" Robin protested. "You're actually going to show this to Dan? This guy sells *cancer* insurance!"

"Look," I said. "If no one can remember the name of the company, if no one wants to think about insurance, if every other competitor in the category is counting on fuzzy sentimentality—then a funny duck with attitude might be just the ticket. We're capitalizing on the very thing that Dan can't stand: The name is impossible to remember!"

We put our top choices, including the duck ad, in front of focus groups. Four ads tested well—one that used comedian Ray Romano as a spokesperson, one emotional ad, and a couple of humorous commercials. The duck ad was anything but a sure bet: Half the people thought it was hysterically funny, others found it downright insulting.

We knew we had to send the four top-scoring ads to Dan Amos for the official test, but I decided that I couldn't let this duck idea die. I picked up the phone and called Amos.

"Listen, I know you only want four ads, but we've got one more that you really should test. It's kind of a crazy commercial, but it just might work," I told him. I gave him a short description of "Park Bench."

Amos was reluctant to take it. "We've agreed to four, and we really don't want to test a fifth," he said. "And I don't know about this duck."

"I'll tell you what," I pleaded. "We'll even pay for the testing."

Amos remembers thinking to himself, If an advertising agency is willing to pay for the testing, there's gotta be something to this. "Well I guess it's better than a naked man tap-dancing on a roof, so let's do it," he finally agreed.

KTG would pay for the test, and if it was a hit, AFLAC would reimburse KTG the cost.

Amos sent KTG's five ads, plus the other agency's four to Ipsos-ASI, Inc., a worldwide advertising research firm based in Norwalk, Connecticut. Ipsos-ASI showed the ad to a lot of consumers, then tabulated the percentage who could remember the name of the company twenty-four hours later. The result is known as a "recall" score.

Generally speaking, in the insurance category, a score of 12 percent is considered a decent ad. Rarely does an insurance ad do better.

"Park Bench" scored a whopping 28 percent.

It was the highest recall score that Ipsos-ASI had ever seen in the insurance category. KTG won the account.

Dan Amos was the duck's first fan—and, for a while, its *only* fan. "I was so excited about the commercials that I couldn't wait to tell everybody. I called some of my friends and some people in business with me, and I explained that we had a duck that would quack our name. I told them how funny it was. And they looked at me like I was nuts. I finally made the decision that I wouldn't tell anybody, including the board of directors. I decided that what I'd do is let the commercials speak for themselves."

And speak they have. On December 31, 1999, the commercial aired for the first time. Within six days, AFLAC had received more hits on its website than in the entire previous year. KTG went on to create over a dozen more AFLAC commercials starring the frustrated duck. The AFLAC duck aired on the opening ceremony of the 2002 Winter Olympics. AFLAC's annual sales increase, which historically had hovered around 12 to 15 percent, was up 28 percent for the year 2000, 29 percent for 2001. Since the campaign began, the company has experienced a 55 percent increase in sales. Dan Amos, who's taken to wearing duck-adorned ties, recently reminded me, "I *am* somebody because of that duck!"

The duck changed the lives of AFLAC salespeople around the country. AFLAC insurance is primarily sold to human resources managers, and before the duck came on the scene, these managers were indifferent to the cold calls from AFLAC. The duck became what's called a doorknob warmer, and now whenever a salesperson picks up the phone, the human resources person on the other end screams, *"AFLAC! AFLAC!"* The salespeople get in the door nearly every time. And as any salesperson will tell you, getting in is half the battle.

The AFLAC duck has become a pop icon. In February 2002 I had the great honor to be selected as the 2001 Advertising Woman of the Year by the Advertising Women of New York. Dan Amos, who was one of the principal speakers at the lunch, took the opportunity to tell the following anecdote during his speech:

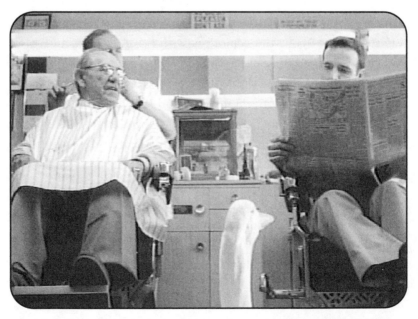

"THEY GIVE YOU CASH, WHICH IS JUST AS GOOD AS MONEY," YOGI PROCLAIMS TO THE BEWILDERMENT OF THE AFLAC DUCK.

"We recently got a call from our research guy, who wanted to speak with me. He said it was very important. I got on the phone and the guy said, 'We have just discovered that 91 percent of all Americans now recognize the name AFLAC. You've got 91 percent name awareness. But that is not why I'm calling you.'

" 'I'm calling you because something happened that has never happened to me before.'

"I said, 'What's never happened?'

"He said, 'One third of the people could not say AFLAC, they had to *quack* it!'"

Dennis Miller has quacked AFLAC on Monday Night Football, and it's been in several syndicated cartoons and the venerable *New York Times* crossword puzzle. When David Pringle, AFLAC's man in D.C., went to a November 2001 White House function, he was introduced to President Bush. Bush took one look at the little duck-pin on his lapel and immediately quacked, "*AFLAC!*"

All of this amounts to literally hundreds of millions of dollars of free advertising. And not just for us. Ben Affleck has jumped on the duck's tail feathers. The duck was compared to Ben in the pages of *People* magazine ("AFLAC spokesduck: Has never laid an egg . . . Ben Affleck: Starred in *Reindeer Games*"). The AFLAC connection has become shtick for Ben's talk-show gigs, where he protests too much about how "the duck haunts me everywhere I go."

There were a million reasons not to use that duck. It used humor in a deadly serious category. It was wacky. It was unconventional. It was naïve. It was impolite. It made fun of the client's anonymity. It stemmed from a random fact: The company's name rhymes with *quack*. It was a last-minute solution. Instinct told us it would work. Fortunately we had the chutzpah to use that duck, and the result is that AFLAC went from virtual anonymity to a household name in one year.

The AFLAC duck wasn't just a random stroke of luck. Big Bangs don't just happen. Creativity is indeed a messy business, but when we developed that campaign we followed some key principles that can help

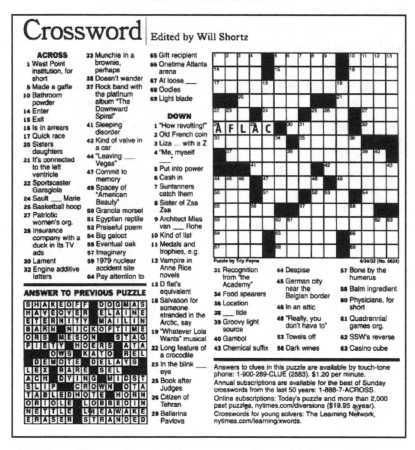

make any marketing department or company fertile ground for Big Bangs.

In the following chapters, you'll learn that Big Bangs are anything but business as usual. You'll learn that, Einstein notwithstanding, energy equals a lean, flat management structure multiplied by emotion, squared. You'll learn that you need to go for the gut, spinning emotional impulse into gold. You'll learn that chaos is the flip side of creativity. You'll learn how to create a condensed environment that moves at warp speed. You'll become expert in recognizing which ideas will work, and which will fizzle. How to execute and sell your Big Bang. How to bust out of black holes, and keep Big Bangs perpetually expanding. In the end, you'll develop the tools to create an immediate and dramatic impact on your company's bottom line.

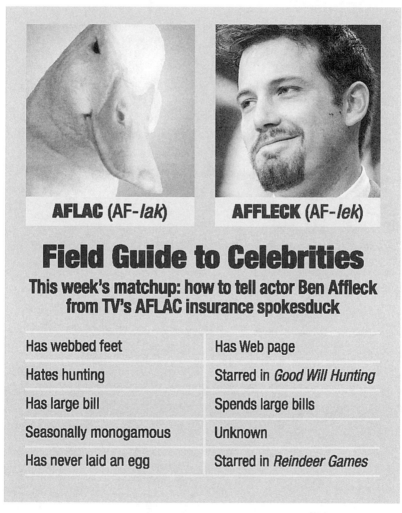

AFLAC (AF-*lak*)   **AFFLECK** (AF-*lek*)

Field Guide to Celebrities

This week's matchup: how to tell actor Ben Affleck from TV's AFLAC insurance spokesduck

Has webbed feet	Has Web page
Hates hunting	Starred in *Good Will Hunting*
Has large bill	Spends large bills
Seasonally monogamous	Unknown
Has never laid an egg	Starred in *Reindeer Games*

SOMETIMES A CAMPAIGN TAKES ON CELEBRITY STATUS—THE BIGGEST BANG OF ALL.

CHAPTER

2

LOSE

The Rules

No one in 1994 thought that a prime-time orgasm could turn a nearly defunct shampoo into a best-selling brand. So when my team first came up with the idea of the "Totally Organic Experience"—which features a woman in the throes of ecstasy every time she uses an Herbal Essences product—just about everybody thought it was inappropriate, outlandish, and wrong. *And that's how I knew it was right.*

At the time, I was working for Wells, Rich, Greene, a New York advertising agency. One of Wells's biggest clients was Procter & Gamble, which owns Pantene, a direct competitor of Herbal Essences. It's common courtesy to show clients any work you do for a competitor, so we played the Herbal ads for P&G. They quickly told me that the ads wouldn't work, dismissing Herbal as a washed-up has-been, no match for Procter & Gamble's best-selling Pantene. I remember, in particular, a top executive at P&G pronouncing, "Your advertising has no demo to show its effectiveness, nor does it have beautiful hair shots. It will never sell one bottle of shampoo. And it will *never* compete with Pantene."

What this executive didn't understand is that the first requirement of a Big Bang is to *forget every rule you ever learned*. In order to disrupt the established paradigm and get the consumer's attention, you need to consider everything *except* the traditional approach. You need to take risks and consider options that no one else has considered. Obviously you don't want to create a campaign that is downright offensive or so irrelevant to the subject at hand that consumers forget what the brand is. But you must have the courage to fly in the face of conventional wisdom and break rules.

Copernicus. Picasso. Eminem. Each one of them broke the rules (as well as a few commandments). Face it, the best you can say about rules is that they make it easy to repeat what others have done before you. Since most of us are not Julia Child, this comes in handy when making a cake. But if all you do is trace somebody else's steps, most of your ideas will be half-baked at best. By definition, rules are backward-looking. Rules anticipate that history will repeat itself. In today's business climate, however, if you keep repeating yourself, your company *is* history.

You cannot be open to suggestions if you rigidly adhere to common assumptions. Suppose someone suggests that you sell cakes made with pickles. The conventional response is: "No, no, no. Cakes don't have pickles." A Big Bang response—after a moment of thought—might be: "Dill or gherkins?" Then, lo and behold, they may turn out to be a hit with pregnant mothers, and sell like, well, hotcakes.

Consider this real-life example of two men who didn't let conventional wisdom get in the way of a good idea. Bruce and Mark Becker, two young guys from Queens, New York, recently opened up an ice cream company. Now, if the Becker brothers had launched a traditional hot-fudge-sundae store, they might have been out of business by the time you read this page. Who needs another ice cream shop? Instead, they did exactly what T. Irene Sanders, executive director of the Washington Center for Complexity and Public Policy and author of *Strategic Thinking and the New*

Science, claims is needed to survive in today's competitive environment. They were able to "abandon overnight those programs, policies and strategies that are outdated or ineffective in the present context." Their outside-the-box idea? Flavors like nova lox and beer-and-nuts ice cream. These guys figured that in our workaday world, the latent thrill-seeker in all of us would pony up for, say, a garlic ice cream cone with sprinkles. We can get our kicks by taking our licks.

They were right. Their business is such a Big Bang that *People* magazine anointed them two of the "most eligible bachelors" for 2002. They were featured in a story in the *New York Times* and appeared on national television as guests on several talk shows, including *Rosie*—and they've been scooping up the profits ever since.

The Big Bang approach to marketing is tailor-made for today's world. Consumers are so inundated with advertising and products that only a disruptive idea will penetrate their consciousness. It's unlikely that any of us will ever be promoting a truly revolutionary product that commands attention all by itself. Thus it's all the more essential that your *message* be revolutionary. And in order to come up with these disruptive, revolutionary, Big Bang messages, you must unravel the conventional clutter in your mind. You must ignore industry standards and turn the following pieces of unconventional wisdom into a way of life.

Forget About the Vision Thing

Too many companies have their five-year plan, their one-year plan, their six-month plan. This stuff rarely works. What's the point of having a vision for what you want to attain in five years, if you can't pay your rent now? A young man named Joyce Hall didn't plan to start a worldwide card company. He just took a train to Kansas City in 1910 with two shoeboxes stuffed with greeting cards, in the hopes of making the world a schmaltzier place. Sam Walton never had a vision. He just wanted to sell small inconsequential items. The kazillion dollars he made was just the happy result. Why limit your potential by instituting some heavy-handed philosophy that only profits the engraver who etches it on the limestone wall you probably overpaid for? It's crucial to avoid "cultural lock-in," say Richard N. Foster and Sarah Kaplan in their best-selling book *Creative Destruction: Why Companies That Are Built to Last Underperform the Market—and How to Successfully Transform Them*. They warn against "the formation of hidden sets of rules, or mental models, that once formed, are extremely difficult to change."

Many great icons of modern culture happened by accident. In their seminal book, *Built to Last: Successful Habits of Visionary Companies,* James C. Collins and Jerry I. Porras studied eighteen major corporations and found that "what looks in retrospect like brilliant foresight and preplanning was often the result of 'Let's just try a lot of stuff and keep what works.'" Some of the best moments on television, for example, were temporary fixes that were never expected to go down in history. Rod Serling was a fill-in spokesperson for *The Twilight Zone* until his producers finally realized that his stilted way of speaking came across as otherworldly and eerie. After Wendy's famous "Where's the beef?" campaign, founder Dave Thomas decided to become the on-air spokesperson until the company could think up another blockbuster campaign. Thomas turned out to be it. *Saturday Night Live* was just supposed to be filler until NBC could come up with something better than reruns of Johnny Carson's *Tonight Show*.

Nowhere is the need to lose the vision thing greater than in marketing. The consumer is a moving target, and in order to capture his or her imagination you must be open to every possibility. A specific vision for your company or brand today could easily be outdated tomorrow. It is the very thing that leads to the same old marketing ideas, whereas a more freewheeling approach enables you to consider out-there ideas that have far more potential to become Big Bangs.

DAVE THOMAS, ORIGINALLY A FILL-IN, BECAME AN ICON FOR THE BRAND.

If you have a vision, you live in a future that is predetermined by the past. If you don't have a vision, you create in the *here and now* (although we've been in some tough meetings where we wished we could magically transport ourselves into the following week). You react to the present without the restrictions of a high-minded corporate mission. Our first business cards were purposefully vague, flashing a colorful cartoon logo and the words "Advertising and Entertainment Company." This broad moniker basically assured prospective clients that we could handle any assignment short of bypass surgery and piloting photo-reconnaissance planes. In fact, this lack of philosophy helped us to produce one of our most applauded Big Bangs, a TV special for the American Red Cross.

Blood . . . Sweat and Tears

In 1998 the American Red Cross asked us to create a new public service announcement to boost its support for its life-saving services. Knowing that most PSAs typically air at about 3 A.M., I felt that the organization deserved more. We needed something bigger, something more disruptive. Then one day I was hit with inspiration.

"I've got it," I announced as I walked into Robin's office one morning. "We're gonna do a TV show for the Red Cross."

Robin stared at me blankly. There was *no one* on our staff who had worked in television programming.

"Are you out of your mind?" she asked me. "How?"

The One-Hour Vision

Whenever you feel tempted to escape into the clear, problem-free future, jolt your brain back to the present by setting one-hour goals for your team. Take a sticky problem and pressure the group to solve it in the next sixty minutes. We believe when you deal with today, the future has a way of resolving itself. So while we do budget and plan, we keep our focus on the road immediately in front of us. In fact, we created a year's worth of Herbal Essences commercials doing exactly this exercise.

"I don't know," I replied. "But that's the Big Bang we need. We're gonna do a TV show."

Robin took a deep breath. "OK," she said. "We're gonna do a TV show."

Now, if we were the sort of company that rigidly adhered to a set of specific long-term goals, we would have organized a four-day off-site to discuss the best strategy for evolving our corporate mission to include television. We would have hired several muckety-muck TV industry consultants. We would have immersed ourselves in weeks of planning committee meetings. And we would have discovered that 99 out of every 100 TV scripts never sees the light of day. The idea would have floundered like a fish in Love Canal.

Instead, we just plunged ahead, full of naïve confidence. Think of all the life-saving moments we could re-create, I told Nancy Crozier, then the director of corporate advertising for the American Red Cross. The excitement, the compassion, the gut-wrenching heroic tales of everyday people helped by the services of American Red Cross volunteers and supporters. Crozier agreed. While other production companies had also approached the American Red Cross to do a special, she felt that our concept was exactly the kind of thing that could strengthen the charity's image. Crozier immediately agreed to help make it happen.

When we went to peddle our concept for an uplifting special to the networks, however, we discovered that no one was jumping at the chance to air the show. The basic response was: "A special on the Red Cross? Sure! We'll run it next July at midnight." None of the networks thought they could sell enough advertising to justify airing the show during prime time. I begrudgingly saw their point, but wasn't going to let our project end up competing with late-night infomercials.

Determined to find a prime-time home for our concept, I went back to Crozier. She told us that she was pretty sure the charity could secure support from some of its loyal corporate supporters. With this tentative source of cash in hand, we were able to line up a meeting with Bill Cecil, who was then the head of sales and pre-funded programming at CBS. We managed to sell him on the fact that this show was perfect for a prime-time audience. After all, I said, the *Touched by an Angel* demographic would just eat up all these Good Samaritan stories, and the network would be considered a hero just for airing it.

To get the final approval, however, we needed to guarantee Jack Sussman, the senior vice president of specials, that the show would not be a one-hour infomercial about how to administer CPR. It had to have what no successful TV show lacks: Stars. Five or more of them, in fact. Of course, neither Robin nor I could come up with a single celebrity (unless you count my friend Steven Herbst, who is a world-renowned classical whistler), but that didn't stop us. We asked everyone at KTG to cash in their favors to come up with some names. Lisa Bifulco, who heads our Broadcast and Production division, worked 24/7 with casting agent Kelly Brock to follow through on leads and wrangle commitments. Collaborating with another production company and the American Red Cross, we were eventually able to secure Garth Brooks, Trisha Yearwood, Sinbad, Bill Cosby, and a slew of others.

With this list of celebrities in hand, CBS greenlighted the project (as long as the funding came through) and, in collaboration with two other production companies, we executive-produced the show. It was a series of individual segments, which were each based on a real-life story showing how American Red Cross supporters provide life-saving services in communities all across the country. One story focused on Bill Jenson, a fifty-four-year-old firefighter who fought the horrific 1996 Malibu fires and ended up with burns over sixty percent of his body. He needed over 100 pints of blood in order to survive. Thousands of eager blood donors lined up at an American Red Cross blood drive to help save this man's life. Another segment featured Ruth Easton, who, at the ripe old age of one hundred, had been a Red Cross volunteer since 1917! Each story was introduced by a celebrity, peppering the show with the star quality CBS required. When we viewed the final cuts of the show, we saw it as a good sign that no one could get through a viewing without a Kleenex in hand.

Our final test of the show's merit, however, was when the American Red Cross went to get final approval for the funding. They aired the special for representatives from a few of the charity's major corporate partners. Fortunately, they loved it as much as we did. AT&T and others were thrilled to be associated with the project and immediately signed up as sponsors. Once we got their support, CBS's Sussman gave final approval to run the show during a time when people would be awake. *The American Red Cross Celebrates Real Life Miracles,* hosted by Roma Downy from *Touched by an Angel,* ran at 8 P.M. on December 24, 1998.

For a company that knew as much about producing television

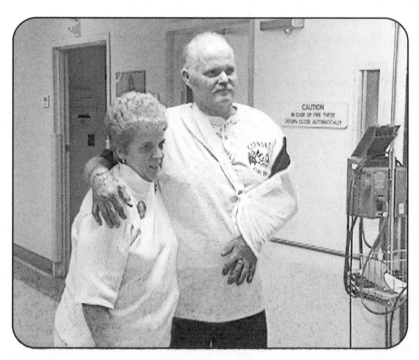

OUR TELEVISION SPECIAL WAS A BIG BANG WAY FOR AMERICA TO SEE THE GOOD WORKS OF THE AMERICAN RED CROSS.

specials as my husband knows about preparing chicken stock, KTG fared well. But if we had started our company with some lofty prophetic vision etched into our psyche, we would have come up with a bunch of great public service announcements for the American Red Cross—and nothing else.

Instead, we opened up new vistas for KTG. We have produced videos for the United Jewish Communities, a documentary about our company (*How to Succeed in Advertising, Without Really Crying*), and political spots for Bill Bradley. We produced a morale-building presentation video, "Crossroads," for the American Red Cross as well, composed by my husband, Fred Thaler, with lyrics by KTG copywriter Robin Schwarz, which won a John Lennon Original Song-Writing Award for best new gospel song. We were able to do all of this because we never focused on any particular vision for our company. As a result, it seemed like the most natural thing in the world to create this Big Bang.

Forget About the Conventional Wisdom

Imagine if the first man-ape who started a fire had decided to focus group the idea with the rest of his clan. Would they have jumped up and cheered, "Hooray! You have just given Homo sapiens its greatest gift. Now we can keep warm, cook our food, and mold sharp pointy tools to kill each other with." No. They would have angrily grunted back: "What's so hot about fire? We can clump together to keep warm, Ulga makes a fabulous mammoth tartare, and if we get invaded by Cave 8 we'll just throw a big rock at them."

It is in our nature to walk down the well-traveled road because it feels safe and comfortable. In every industry, the hordes tend to follow a certain set of rules that are the "gospel" of that particular category. Always show the car mechanic in the muffler ads. Always put size 2 mannequins with size 12 breasts in the shop window. Always describe beige as "oatmeal" in your spring catalog. These traditional business concepts, however, are often the fastest route

When Wrong Is Right

If an idea at first blush seems wrong, stop and examine what it is that makes you so uncomfortable. It could be that it's truly inappropriate and doesn't solve the problem. On the other hand, perhaps no one has ever looked at the problem from that weird under-the-table angle before. Completely logical conclusions result from well-trodden paths that have been traversed by legions of well-meaning marketers. Always examine *why* an idea is being rejected before tossing it out with the evening trash.

to obscurity. IBM's nosedive in the 1980s, according to Foster and Kaplan in *Creative Destruction,* was the result of "a failure to recognize that continuity—business as usual—is a fallacy." Was it Albert Einstein who said, "the definition of insanity is doing the same thing over and over again, each time expecting a different result"?

Behind most great companies are people who ignored the industry standard. Robert McDonald, president of global fabric and home care for Procter & Gamble, says that "in my experience, the really successful things are counterintuitive. Of course you have to be careful. You can't come out with something that doesn't compute at all with the consumer's experience. But if you can take a consumer belief and turn it on its head, it becomes a powerful idea."

Take the superstore concept at Barnes & Noble. Every MBA graduate will tell you that stores should be designed to get customers in and out, in short order, to make room for the next customer. In the late 1980s, Leonard Riggio, the longtime chairman of Barnes & Noble, came up with a brilliant marketing move by deciding to focus on the opposite: Get the customer to stay awhile. He instinctively knew that Barnes & Noble could sell a lot more books if his stores became oases of calm and contemplation in a world spinning madly out of control. He became the first bookseller in the country to pour his resources into a chain of superstores that had the ambience of a local library. B&N's trademark hunter-green carpeting, stuffed chairs, walnut-stained bookshelves, cafés, and magazine racks invite you to wander the offerings, latte in hand, for hours. Riggio envisioned the stores as community centers that sponsored author's readings, lecture series, and concerts. Even kids were encouraged to linger. In your average shop, kids are about as welcome as a bear in an ICU. Barnes & Noble created evening programs where toddlers were invited to show up with their blankies and listen to bedtime stories.

The result of all this down-home good cheer? Barnes & Noble eclipsed the competition, and became the largest bookseller in the country, with over 900 stores in 49 states.

Another case in point: What's the bottom line at discount retailers like Kmart & Wal-Mart? The bottom line. Price first, design last. Target has turned that around. While they don't ignore price, they hired cutting-edge designers like Todd Oldham and Stephen Sprouse to create designer alarm clocks and bathing suits for the company's shelves. Until Target came along, people went to discount stores because they wanted the best deal. Period. But the creative minds at Target realized that it's not only rich people who like to be hip. The store has become so identified with cool design that it has earned the Frenchifying moniker "Tar-jay." The company now runs TV commercials where the name of the store is never even seen or mentioned; all you see is the signature bull's-eye logo. Remember the day when Kmart filed for bankruptcy? Target's stock price was up 19 percent from the previous year.

Forget About Fear

Let's face it: No risk, no bang. Every Big Bang has been created by someone who has risked big time. The Pilgrims sailed off in ships that would fit in a duck pond. Rosa Parks sat in the front of the bus. Charles Lindbergh flew east. Somebody, somewhere, ate that first piece of garlic. When Dan Amos, the chairman of AFLAC, saw "Park Bench," our first duck commercial, his first thought was: "How in the hell am I going to tell my board of directors?"

Most people think that business is all about doing enough research to take risk out of the equation. Sure, if your brother-in-law wants $20 million for his new infomercial, you should do due diligence to see if the world is ready for a do-it-yourself dentistry kit. You have to know the rules before you can break them.

> ### Don't Overanalyze
>
> Knowing too much about a company can blind you to a Big Bang idea. Isn't it ironic when a client asks you to take a look at his or her business with fresh eyes, and then proceeds to plunk a 250-page briefing book on your desk? Of course, the truth is, you need to do both—study the business and bring fresh eyes to the table— but in the right order. First, jot down your initial impressions, thoughts, and feelings upon beginning the project. Valuable insights and associations come to the surface when you know very little about a business, because you are seeing the product or brand the way the consumer does. *Then* read the briefing book and do your homework. Nine times out of ten, after we've absorbed a tome's worth of background information about the brand, we find our Big Bang in our earliest notes.

But marketing isn't like building a Hubble Space Telescope. Sometimes having a few loose screws can give you a wider view of what's possible, while knowing too much about the nuts and bolts of every issue can weigh down your creative flight, and obscure the underlying and essential issues. Let's face it. If women were required to do a dissertation on motherhood before they got pregnant, planet Earth would be one empty rotating parking lot. No woman without a straitjacket would merrily go through labor if she knew it was going to feel like being impaled on a steak knife (no wonder the word *epidural* ignites emotions more intense than the act of procreation itself). Luckily for the human race, none of us have been "thoroughly thought through."

Courage means living with uncertainty. It means trying something new—even if there's a potential downside. As Procter & Gamble CEO A. G. Lafley recently told us, "The trouble with big companies is they'll go for the safe, comfortable middle. You don't get anywhere if you go into the safe, comfortable middle. You have to keep edging out."

The worst thing you can do is remain static, as IBM discovered in the 1980s. Concentrating on the business they had built—mainframe computers—they were unwilling to risk a venture into desktop models. While this was happening, says Elspeth McFadzean, a behavioral scientist at Henley Management College in England, new companies such as Compaq, Intel, and Microsoft started focusing on personal computers. "Consequently, by the early 1990s, IBM had lost market share together with $15 billion." You've got to screw up the nerve to "look forward and to explore more dynamic, creative solutions," says McFadzean.

An example of courageously heading into uncharted territory is when Peter Schweitzer, who ran the Detroit outpost of the J. Walter Thompson advertising agency in the 1980s, suggested to Ford Motor Company that it should market its cars to women. Until that point, car commercials were directly primarily at men, often with buxom babes sprawling over the hood while a male voiceover talked about the car. The folks at Ford started to realize that women are often the biggest decision makers in the household when it comes to consumer purchases. So they hired Susan Lucci to pitch the cars to women. It was the first time that a female spokesperson was selected to sell cars in a major television campaign, and it was extremely successful, according to Schweitzer.

Pen Envy

One Big Bang that took a lot of nerve was our campaign for Trumbull, Connecticut–based Pilot Pen. In early 2001 Pilot Pen was a distant number three in the gel-ink pen category. This was unacceptable, as far as they were concerned, and they asked us to help them change things around. This was no small task. Pens are considered commodities. Many people tend to buy the cheapest one they can find; they further demonstrate their disinterest in their pen by promptly losing it. Pilot Pen's new Dr. Grip gel-ink pens are significantly more expensive than its competitors' low-priced products, and the challenge was to convince consumers to buy the expensive brand name. The kicker? CEO Ron Shaw told us that the company wanted to see a big increase in sales just *six weeks* after the ads aired. Oh, and their budget was under $5 million.

We knew that the advertising would need to be very intrusive to get noticed, and convincing enough to get people to buy. Now for those of you not familiar with a Dr. Grip, let us elaborate on its fine points. Dr. Grip pens have a thick-sized barrel, making them easy to grasp for all you large, manly men out there. The bottom half of the barrel is molded from a deep cushiony silicone material, creating a writing tool that even makes signing your mortgage check pleasurable.

Robin simply loved, *loved,* her Dr. Grip. From the moment she began writing with it (Robin fondly recollects she was scribbling the word *declined* on an expense report at the time), she began to exhibit strange territorial tendencies toward her pen. She never left it out of her sight, and one day she admitted to me that she had gone out and bought refills for it! Now that was obsessive behavior as far as I was concerned. But soon everybody on the pitch began to exhibit this same odd possessiveness toward his or her Dr. Grip. Some even tried to lock up their offices at night, a pathetic ploy, since they worked in an open space.

But this possessive behavior led us to pursue a strategic direction to a Big Bang idea. It was an idea so clear, so bold, so brazen, that even Dr. Freud would get the point: *When you write with a Dr. Grip, everyone around you has pen envy.*

We feverishly started stealing each other's Dr. Grip pens and began to write until all hours of the night. Like any really Big Bang idea, the concept generated myriad scripts, one funnier than the next. But the spot I really longed to do, the truly disruptive "I can't believe this is on the air" commercial, was one I came up with that I was sure would never see the light of day. In fact, no one actually believed I'd have the guts to show it.

When we went to present our ideas to the Pilot Pen folks, our team had gathered in a boardroom expansive enough to have its own zip code, surrounded by a sea of men in suits. Everyone was a bit nervous. We were the last of several agencies to present, and who knew if they had already fallen hopelessly in love with another campaign? They could have gone bananas over some snappy jingle they heard—after all, there are a lot of words out there that rhyme with "pen." But we brazenly unzipped our portfolios, and began to present our scripts.

Ron Shaw seemed quite taken with many of them—probably because they were a significant step up from some of the previous campaigns (although he *was* partial to one where he delivered his pitch from a man's shirt pocket). After about an hour or so, most of the KTG team felt that the presentation had gone so well that we were ready to pack up our boards and head on home. But I thought that Mr. Shaw seemed so receptive to our edgy ideas that he might be willing to go even one step further.

Glancing up, I could see Rob Snyder, our senior art director on the pitch, pleading the words *"no, no, no"* at me with his eyes. Still, since Pilot Pen had a budget that would fit into the back pocket of a Levi's shrink-to-fit jean, I knew that they needed copy that would stop a remote in its tracks. So I gingerly picked up the last remaining board, and read the following:

> *Two guys sitting next to each other on the train, viewed only from the chest up.*
>
> *First guy, staring at the lap of the second guy with admiration:* Wow. Some instrument you got there.
>
> *Second guy, raising an eyebrow:* Like it?
>
> *First, sighing:* Yeahhh. So—
>
> *Second:* Impressive?
>
> *First:* Yeah! Must give you great joy.
>
> *Second:* You wanna hold it?
>
> *First, breathlessly:* Could I?
>
> *Second, handing over the pen, which finally comes into view:* That's why they call it Dr. Grip.

After they regained consciousness, they all started to howl with laughter. Shaw exclaimed, "It's outrageous, it's daring, and it will probably get us a ton of negative letters, but it's just the punch we need." A week later, against a pitch of five other agencies, we were awarded the business.

"Train" aired along with another humorous, but much less daring, commercial. Although it only ran for a few weeks, it created so much publicity that one viewing was all any consumer needed. And for the first time, Pilot Pen advertising got a full story in the *New York Times*. No less important, Pilot Pen captured the number-one gel-ink pen position during the crucial back-to-school period, and their sales jumped 31 percent after just six weeks of advertis-

"PEN ENVY": THERE'S NOTHING MORE SATISFYING THAN HOLDING A DR. GRIP
IN YOUR HANDS.

ing—much to the envy of those who held anything less satisfying in their hands.

So there you have the three crucial components of a Big Bang mindset: Stay in the here and now. Stick to the road not taken. Be fearless. This is all you need to break rules with gusto.

Perhaps the best argument for this unorthodox philosophy is the story of the Herbal Essences "Totally Organic Experience" campaign. Remember the Breck girl? She was the classic shampoo model: A pretty, wholesome girl with long beautiful hair who just smiled and shook her shimmering locks. She never did anything controversial. In 1994, it was common knowledge that this was the only way to sell shampoo. But I knew that the only way to sell a shampoo teetering on the edge of oblivion was to go in the opposite direction. As a result, we came up with an idea that bucked

> **Don't Get Stuck in the Process Trap**
>
> Don't focus on *how* things get done at the expense of actually getting things done. We never have meetings to talk about how a project should get done, and, whenever possible, we make a decision instead of scheduling a meeting to talk about making a decision. We try not to have an agenda with more than three items on it. We are loath to add rules to any process unless we absolutely have to. Less process means more progress.

every trend. It required a giant dose of chutzpah from every person along the chain of command. And it was wildly successful.

As we revisit the Herbal story in detail, you'll see how turning your back on conventional wisdom can be a launching pad to a Big Bang.

The Orgasm Felt 'Round the World

One cold November morning in 1994, I got a call from Steve Sadove, the president of Clairol. The company was going to reintroduce Herbal Essences shampoo. Clairol had been considering pulling the brand from the shelves, but had decided to give it one more shot at survival. They'd revamped the whole product, giving it a stronger new fragrance and snappy new packaging. Sadove complained to me, however, that the advertising being developed to promote the new shampoo was dull, flat, and lifeless. Sadove asked if I would be willing to find a way to excite consumers about the relaunch of what began as a hippie hair-care product. With a budget of $10 million, in a category where a $50 million media buy is the price of entry, he knew he needed advertising that would explode onto the scene.

Clairol had first launched Herbal Essences in the early seventies. Those of you old enough to remember (if you are wearing reading glasses right now, that would be you) will recall that blissful time of Earth Shoes, Save the Whales, and "I Can't Get No Satisfaction." Herbal Essences was the first big brand to use natural ingredients and a botanical fragrance. The tag line was "Enter the Garden of Earthly Delights." It was the right idea at the right time, and the brand quickly became a top seller. Unfortunately it languished during the eighties when natural was out, and junk bonds and shoulder pads were in. It was about to be discontinued when the nineties brought a second wave of natural fever with brands like The Body Shop, Bath & Body Works, and Aveda.

The trouble was, Sadove's advertising agency had been working unsuccessfully on this relaunch for a year (that's a lot of bad hair days), and Clairol was up against an air date they couldn't miss. Coincidentally, Robin was running the account at Clairol's agency, losing sleep over the fact that another agency was now pitching it. By the time Sadove made the call to me, we only had five days to develop the campaign. Four of them were over the Thanksgiving holiday.

It seemed like an impossible assignment, but I have found that I am often my most creative when I am working within tight constraints. It's like writing haiku. The form is so strict that there is no room for deviation. From out of the smallest windows often flow the freshest ideas.

The first thing I did was eliminate anyone on the team who had worked on shampoo advertising. I didn't want anything that remotely resembled the usual hair fare. No luminous, slo-mo hair drop shots (Pantene owned that visual), no blond beauty with collagen lips pouting over her dried-out "before" tresses, and no beads of vitamins rushing to rescue and resuscitate damaged follicles. This had to be advertising that made your hair stand on end, so to speak, not swing seductively back and forth.

In other words, in order to break the "Breck" mold, we had to forget everything we had ever learned about shampoo advertising. The newly designed Herbal Essences bottle, brilliantly conceived by John Louise, a former vice president at Clairol, was a good place to start for inspiration. It was unique in its natural look and texture. It was made of clear plastic, so that the distinctive color for each shampoo formulation (for oily, dry, or limp hair) was visible. On the back of the bottle there was a listing of the product's all-natural herbs and botanicals, adorned with an inviting floral image. But the true stroke of brilliance was the fact that the floral image emanated right through the shampoo. It gave you the impression of a fresh flower growing right in the bottle, a botanical feat even Mother Nature would have found impressive. When you open up a bottle of Herbal Essences, the sweet, aromatic scent of herbs is like an olfactory romp through a Martha Stewart nursery, making the product invitingly pleasurable to use.

Knowing that all shampoo advertising focused on the end result of shiny, silky, "no way you'll ever get this unless you're Polynesian" hair, our account planner, Douglas Atkin, suggested that we disrupt the norm for the category. Maybe, just maybe, he started telling everyone, there was some *other* reason to wash your hair.

Well, most of us knew that just about any shampoo would get your hair clean. But how did women feel about the act of shampooing itself? Apparently no one had ever asked them *that* question. Perhaps if we talked to women about shampooing, we'd get somewhere. It was already Friday, however, and we had a meeting with Clairol the following Tuesday. With no time to set up anything as formal as a focus group, we did some guerrilla research and debriefed every woman in the agency about washing her hair.

What we learned was that although women initially groused that shampooing was a boring chore, further questioning revealed that it was actually a revitalizing and sensual experience. In fact, many women realized that it was often the best five minutes of their day. No kids nagging them, no grumpy husband asking where his blue shirt is, nothing but a lather of soapy suds washing away the petty problems of life. And they admitted there was something deeply sensual about it. They were naked, they were massaging their scalps, they were feeling a rush of pulsating hot water all over their bodies—well, you get the idea.

So we decided to go where no hair-care company had gone before: into the shower. And the fragrant scent, the herbs and botanicals awash in pure, mountain spring water, all promised a great shampoo experience.

But the scripts we came up with were as interesting as reruns on the weather channel. We had clips of women romping through fields of poppies, which had the same effect on viewers that they did on Dorothy in *The Wizard of Oz*. We had women diving into waterfalls. We even had women dancing spasmodically in the shower, sort of a *Flashdance* with suds, but it was a far cry from a breakthrough campaign.

On Monday morning I met with one of my best teams, Lynn Blumenfeld and Jim Johnson, who trudged into my office with long faces. "We slaved over this all weekend, and came up with nothing," Lynn blurted out with tears in her eyes. Instead of asking them to do more work, I invited them to stay and talk. I began to joke around, a useful technique to trick the mind into relaxing.

Then I mentioned that if they didn't come up with an idea, maybe we could find a celebrity to hawk the product, to fool the audience into thinking that there really was an idea. One celebrity who came to mind was Meg Ryan, who was attractive, approachable, and funny. The idea made Jim remember the famous scene in *When Harry Met Sally,* when Meg Ryan feigns an orgasm in a coffee shop to an appropriately embarrassed Billy Crystal. As we laughed over the memory, Jim offhandedly said, "I'll have the shampoo she's using."

I suddenly felt a chill.

"Wait a second—that's it!" I blurted out.

"That's what?" Lynn asked.

"That's the idea! We'll show a woman getting into the shower, and she'll have a veritable orgasm washing her hair with Herbal Essences. As she reaches an ecstatic climax over her just washed tresses, we'll cut to a frumpy couple watching her on their television set. The woman will turn to her couch-potato husband, and say, 'I want the shampoo she's using.'"

Lynn and Jim shook their heads in disbelief. "Linda," they argued, "Clairol will *never* buy that. They're owned by Bristol-Myers Squibb, one of the most conservative pharmaceutical companies in America. Even their ads for Excedrin won't show a woman opening her mouth to swallow!"

But I persisted. The next day we presented the concept to Steve Sadove, who loved it. *Yes,* it was sensual, *yes*, it was daring, and *yes* it overpromised more than an Arthur Andersen spreadsheet, but this was the home run he had been hoping for. He asked his marketing people to take a look at the ad. Many of them, Sadove discovered, thought it was in bad taste, not appropriate, and didn't want to do it.

"But I had a gut reaction that this was great stuff, even if it meant I would never see the end of the negative mail," he recalls. He did take one unusual precaution. Before he tested the ad, he showed it to Charlie Heimbold and Dick Gelb, the top brass at Bristol-Myers Squibb. Ordinarily, the buck stopped with Sadove, but this ad was explosive, to say the least. He wanted to make sure that his bosses wouldn't object. Somehow Sadove convinced them that *only an orgasm could save this brand.*

Sadove then quickly sent the commercial out for testing. Clairol's advertising traditionally rated a recall score of 20 to 25. The first Herbal ad scored in the 40s; the second, an eye-opening 67. The "Totally Organic Experience" ads went on to receive the highest test scores of any Clairol spot to date.

Nine years and umpteen commercials later, Herbal Essences has been successfully launched in over 62 countries around the world, and has expanded into body washes, candles, hair color, you name it. Imitation being the sincerest form of flattery, the campaign has

Hope you have as much fun

on your birthday as they do on

that shampoo commercial

"YES! YES! YES!" SCREAMED THE SALES RESULTS WHEN THE HERBAL
ESSENCES SPOT HIT THE AIRWAVES. AS THIS BIRTHDAY CARD DEMONSTRATES,
THE ADS HAVE SECURED A PERMANENT PLACE IN POP CULTURE.

been parodied on every show imaginable, even spawning a birthday card. The commercials have generated the highest awareness of any shampoo advertising in the history of marketing. Advertising for Herbal Essences is now airing in China—soon the brand will be a major hit in this country of over a billion people. In short work, Herbal Essences expanded from a nearly extinct shampoo to the number-two hair-care brand in America.

We created a Big Bang that helped to turn Herbal Essences into one of the fastest growing brands in the world. And we did it because we had the courage to forget everything we were taught and to break all the rules.

Adopting this frame of mind is the first step in pointing your marketing team or company in the direction of Big Bang thinking. The next move is to focus on creating an environment predisposed to coming up with explosive, disruptive ideas.

SHRINK TO
SUCCESS

Big Bang ideas come from small spaces. It is only through shrinking your organization that you can create an atmosphere where great ideas continually bubble up to the surface. We call it the compression theory of marketing. Just as if you were reducing a sauce on your stove, you want to boil time, space, and bureaucracy down so that only the essential elements are left. This will keep your company moving at a fever pitch, ready and able to respond instantly to new developments, and constantly churning out good ideas.

A perfect example of how a compressed office becomes a cauldron of creativity happened one morning in early 1997, during my last few months at Wells, Rich, Greene. I was reading the newspaper in a cab on the way to work, and saw that Dolly the sheep had been cloned. A giant lightbulb went off in my head. I couldn't get to the office fast enough. When I dashed out of the elevator doors into the foyer I was a woman with a mission. Waving the newspaper article in everybody's face, I said over and over that we had to do an ad on cloning. About two minutes after I got to my desk, the phone rang. It was Sally Goll Beatty, a reporter at the *Wall Street*

Journal, who'd spoken to Wells's public relations director, Jan Sneed.

"I'm calling up agencies to see who's doing a cloning ad," she said. "Whoever does the first ad gets the story."

"Well, your story's going to be about us," I responded, hung up the phone, and ran out of my office.

I went to every creative director and told them to stop *immediately* what they were doing and call up clients to see who was willing to do a cloning ad. "Tell them there's a *Journal* column in the offing," I told everyone. "It doesn't matter where the ad runs. It can run in the *Free Press.* We don't need a huge campaign. We just need *one ad.*"

I paced up and down the hallways until I heard someone holler, "Heineken says they're interested!" Steve Davis, vice president of marketing at Heineken and a client of Wells at the time, had given the go-ahead for us to come up with something.

Within minutes I crowded every person I could find into my office, from the most senior creative writer to the most junior assistant. People were sitting on the floor, on tables, the arms of chairs, as we started throwing around ideas. We soon had a bunch of contenders, and about two hours later faxed Davis our favorites.

As eager as we were for the free PR, Davis soon faxed back his approval for the following: An image of two Heineken red stars, side by side, with the tagline, "Which one's the clone? Scary, isn't it?" The ad ran in *Time Out New York* and *Entertainment Weekly.* And sure enough, Sally Goll Beatty published her column, "'How I Got That Idea': Wells, Rich Acts on the Double to Create Clone Ad for Heineken," in the March 18, 1997, issue of the *Wall Street Journal.*

By dropping everything and forcing everyone into action, we generated a blast of publicity. It was an unorthodox route to take. A lot of agencies would have rejected working on the cloning idea because it disrupted the work at hand. Many clients didn't want to do it because it wasn't a part of any strategic long-term plan. But Steve Davis didn't waste a lot of time wondering how a cloning ad

But which one's the clone?

(Scary, isn't it?)

IT'S ALL TRUE

Heineken

True to the original recipe since 1886

http://www.heineken.com
Heineken USA, Inc., White Plains, NY

BREAKING A TOPICAL AD "ON THE DOUBLE" CAN GIVE A BRAND A WEALTH OF
FREE PUBLICITY.

would make Heineken the beer of choice. He realized that while a
single ad was unlikely to spur an enormous jump in sales, that
wasn't the point. It was a great marketing opportunity. It was a
short-term move that created a Big Bang fuss.

It was also a move that can happen only in a company that is small enough to be opportunistic. Without excessive bureaucracy slowing us down, we were able to take a thought on the way to work and make it a business proposition by lunchtime.

Shrinking your company to a nimble organization is the only way to create Big Bangs in today's competitive marketplace. In a 1995 article in the *Journal for Quality and Participation,* the authors note the dangers of moving too slowly: "Knowing one's position in the marketplace is of little comfort when new competitors can appear from out of nowhere, or when your market can be redefined nearly overnight. Think about what happened to the producers of carbon paper and Wite-Out when photocopiers and desktop computers became commonplace." In other words, the only constant in the current economic climate is change.

Here's how we create an organization that is opportunistic and fast enough to create Big Bangs in today's fast-paced world.

Shrink the Space

What's one of the first things people do when they start a business? They look for a comfortable space they can grow into. And that's their first mistake. The amount of extra space is inversely proportioned to creative output. We isolated this principle largely by accident, however, since our first cramped quarters were simply the result of my Jewish frugality gene.

The Kaplan Thaler Group started out in the third floor of my brownstone on Nineteenth Street in Manhattan. A revamped former play space for our kids, it was plenty big enough for the five employees who were there on opening day. Within six months, however, we had won several new accounts and seventeen people were crammed into seven hundred square feet. Prime real estate was an area on the floor where you had your own little space *and* a phone. We were reduced to playing a macabre version of musical chairs, vying for one of the seats every time someone went to the bathroom. We had no storage space, so we kept all our presentation boards in the bathtub, with a big sign that screamed, "*Don't turn on!*"

While I was the first to admit—OK, the last—that a tiny office has its downside, we did discover a very important thing: Ideas permeated every inch of our two-room space. We discovered that when people are close together, they think faster, they work faster, and they focus faster. At one point Clairol asked us to jazz up a mediocre Herbal Essences body-wash commercial that had already been produced by another agency. We quickly agreed, and convinced a freelance editor to haul her video equipment up the three flights to our office. No one could possibly concentrate on anything else, as this project pretty much dominated the whole space.

So we all dropped what we were doing and took a look at the film that had been produced. We gave ourselves about five minutes to rewrite it, which we did improv style by throwing lines at each other. In a couple of hours we edited a very funny spot, and wowed our Clairol client with it the next morning. It aired that week on national television, and a week later we were awarded the whole body-wash business. The ad helped Herbal Essences to become the second leading body-wash brand in America at the time.

KTG is a living testament to the upside of close quarters. In our first claustrophobic office we started out with one client and ended up with a roster that included Toys "R" Us, Aussie, Daily Defense, the American Red Cross, and Bristol-Myers Squibb. We went from $27 million in billings to $100 million in only four months.

Of course, we aren't advocating that you move your company into a closet. When we got to the point where we couldn't answer the phone without knocking someone's coffee on the floor, we decided to move. Three moves and four years later, KTG absorbed N. W. Ayer, arguably America's oldest advertising agency, and inherited several of its clients. This expansion forced us to move into Ayer's thirty-fourth-floor space in World Wide Plaza in Manhattan. Although we're now in offices we could only have dreamed of five years ago, we still maintain the spirit of that third-floor crowding

> ### Cramp Your Style
> Whenever you schedule a creative meeting, don't be afraid to position people so that they are almost uncomfortably close. We also caution against holding creative meetings in formal rooms across huge mahogany tables. Distance can create barriers to spontaneity and interaction; it makes it easy for people to withdraw and doodle their way into oblivion. We make a point of always having one or two fewer chairs than people. Invariably, the guy standing in the corner or sitting on the floor will come up with some of the best ideas.

experiment. We rarely have creative meetings in the conference room, instead cramming everybody into my office. We often serve lunch to keep everyone nearby. People share offices, and we try to keep everyone as close together as possible.

It's important not to confuse the idea of clustering people together with putting them all in an open-office environment, a trend that's hot now even with the most conservative companies. The new Procter & Gamble offices in Singapore, for instance, have done away with individual offices altogether. There are no permanent offices at all. Everyone gets a desk to sit at each day when they sign in, all communication is by cell phone and laptop, and each person has a small rollable cabinet for storing personal items. There are several "huddle" rooms, where people congregate to work on projects together. Open offices like this have advantages, to be sure: It costs less, for one thing, and researchers have found that teams who work in open "war rooms" tend to be more creative than workers in traditional offices.

But we would argue that building teamwork isn't based necessarily on open or closed offices, per se; rather, it's important to have people working *right on top of each other*. Maybe the discomfort motivates people to work faster (some companies actually have meetings standing up for this sole purpose), or because too much space dissipates ideas. When staff members invade each other's territory, they can't seem to help making suggestions, and often those spontaneous critiques improve the work. A byproduct of this casual collaboration is that when the project is completed, many people feel they were integral to its success.

When we moved to our most recent offices, creative team Tom Amico and Eric David opted to share a modest-sized space, even when they were given the choice of having separate offices. "We're more creative when we're in the same room," says Tom. "It's easier to bounce on idea off someone who's on the other end of the carpet rather than the hallway. In general, you want to have as few walls as possible when it comes to thinking up ideas. Sheetrock could be an impediment."

Another unexpected benefit of a crowded office is that there isn't a lot of time spent worrying over office politics: You can't talk behind someone's back because they're right in front of you. There's nowhere to hide and tune out. Your employees spend a lot less time on personal stuff if they're right in the middle of things. It's a little difficult to shop online when your monitor can be seen by five other people. Instead, people focus on the work at hand.

There remains, of course, the issue of convincing your staff that sharing offices, or eliminating private offices altogether, is the way to go. Expansive offices are still traditionally considered a perk in business, and it can be difficult to get staffers to embrace a crowded office concept. In the beginning, our staff complained to us that they couldn't concentrate with so many people wandering in and out, that they overhear everyone else's conversations, that if they bounce a check, everyone will know.

Ravi Chaturvedi, now the Procter & Gamble vice president for health and beauty care in China, was the executive in Singapore who oversaw the move to an open office. He solved the ego problem by making sure it looked like an upgrade. "We had a group at various levels who worked with the designer and who came up with the office design," Chaturvedi says. "People would come look at it and make comments. We emphasized that the open office was part of a cultural tool. We framed it as a cultural intervention, to become the kind of organization we wanted to be. An open, transparent environment, not hiding behind screens. We also created little coffee corners and sofa corners around the office, so people could just chat."

It's all a matter of getting used to it. Dr. Ona Robinson, a New York psychologist and management consultant, suggests that people can learn to flourish in a crowded office. "In a Japanese home," she says, "although you may see a lot of space, you have very little privacy because the walls are very thin. So what they've learned to do as a culture is to become relatively inscrutable. They've built an interior space inside of themselves. Now in our culture, when you put people in an open space, they haven't built interior spaces for privacy. We're taught to go behind closed doors to think. We don't have the skills to work openly.

"The capacity to become civilized, after all, is the capacity to inhibit response to stimulation," she continues. "If you stood in a room and were sensitive equivalently to every bit of stimulus that came at you, you would go crazy. When you put people in an open space, their brains haven't modified to that yet. They can't inhibit a lot of the stimuli that's coming at them. But in the course of time, in spite of their griping, they will develop those skills." Research has borne this out. Judith Olson, a psychology professor at the University of Michigan who has researched open offices, found that workers liked working in one large "war room" more than they expected to, and that they didn't get as distracted by each other as much as they thought they would.

Indeed, as time went on, everyone at KTG became much more comfortable with being in close quarters. In fact, they have become masters at filtering out the background noise of any unrelated banter, while allowing the constant stream of creative sparks that fly out to fan the flames of their own ideas.

Shrink the Hierarchy

When it comes to creating ideas, the last thing you want is seven lines of command. A marketing group or company that expects to produce Big Bangs must be structured with as few supervisors as possible. It is only with a flat management structure, where just a few people hold the reins of power, that creative ideas can flourish and grow.

Say a writer has a great Big Bang idea, which, by its very nature, is offensive or risky to someone. If you have a cumbersome bureaucracy in place, your writer will realize that the the most ef-

Cut the Bureaucracy

Remember the well-dressed woman's favorite trick? Get dressed for the evening, look in the mirror, and take one accessory off. Well, the same is true for hierarchy. Take a good look at your organization and see if you can cut one level. Having fewer levels of hierarchy forces people to *do* rather than *supervise.* Sure, everyone will end up wearing multiple hats. But that's a good thing. Everyone is constantly forced to look at problems from multiple perspectives and less inclined to hand off a project. When a senior staffer needs to be in more than one place at one time, she can send a junior person in her place. We find that, invariably, the junior person does a great job, grows in experience and responsibility, and often can take over that task from then on.

ficient course of action is not to upset the apple cart. Instead of pushing this great idea through all the red tape, he may just think, "Why rock the boat? Someone up the line will eventually kill it anyway." So he'll write an ad or report that no one will hate, choosing the path of least resistance.

It's also the path to mediocrity. What you end up with is an idea that gets through the red tape, but doesn't go through the roof. Excessive bureacracy systematically weeds out Big Bang ideas.

Obviously there are some companies and industries where a formal, hierarchical structure is important. Scientists rely on rigorous peer scrutiny before they can publish a word. Some branches of government need to have several layers of approval to ensure that every constituent is heard. And, of course, every company needs final arbiters on decisions. But even some of the biggest corporations, including AFLAC and our parent company, Publicis Groupe, have a very short chain of command. With a flat management structure, your staff will spend much more time coming up with ideas than approving them.

One way to keep the hierarchy flat is to *stop promoting people*. In most companies the only way to get more money and prestige is to get promoted. We believe that companies need to break the cycle of creating layers of people who yearn to supervise and get a longer title. Promotion can backfire: What good is a terrific writer if he or she now has to spend the day supervising junior writers? Picasso never wanted to become a museum director. Midori isn't angling to become the Berlin Philharmonic's next conductor. The last thing you should do is promote a great writer to executive vice president and tell him that he's going to manage all the other writers. Everyone will end up unhappy. Leadership and creativity are two very different abilities, and it is the rare person who's good at both.

We advocate *horizontal advancement rather than vertical ascension*. Like a great actor who broadens his talents by playing many diverse roles, or an accomplished musician who continually expands her repertoire, your staff should come to understand that their true worth comes from developing their best abilities. Moving up a ladder can easily lead to a place where one's greatest gifts are never used.

Everyone seems to think that empowering the staff is the best route to innovation. According to management consultants Joseph H. Boyett and Henry P. Conn, authors of *Workplace 2000: The Revolution Reshaping American Business,* there is a trend toward self-management in American companies, where teams have no traditional boss or supervisor. Instead, team members take responsibility for their own work. This self-empowered concept may work well in some industries, but not, in our eyes, in marketing. We believe that if you shoulder all the responsibility, you free people to create.

When you delegate power, you delegate responsibility, and responsibility doesn't always beget creativity. When people have to take total control of their projects, they tend to hesitate to try something that has a high risk of failure. But it is precisely those risky ideas that have Big Bang potential. We've found that we limit risk avoidance on the part of our staff by taking the stress out of making a decision. As a result, we get better ideas on the table. People will only come up with a Big Bang idea if they know they don't have to take the heat if it fails.

When KTG was merged with N. W. Ayer, I had a meeting with the Ayer staff and said, "All your titles are going to be taken away because we don't have these titles at KTG. I'm not going to pay you or give you raises according to how many people you supervise. I'm going to reward you for the work you create. It's all about your value to the company." We explained that the real purpose of titles is to describe what you do, not how important you are. Robin and I were worried about the fallout from this decree, but with only a few minor squabbles, we got through it unscathed. Now everyone has a functional title that says what he or she does, like "account director," or "copywriter," but we don't have a string of vice presidents and executive vice presidents.

When employees stop focusing on relatively meaningless rewards like titles, they start to focus on rewards that count, like coming up with a great idea that brings in business. Instead of striving for that promotion, they focus on what they are doing right in the present. The reward isn't always just out of reach; it's there if you get the job done now. Pretty soon your staff will get addicted to that feeling of having a really good day at work. And the more you get that feeling, the more you want it. By forcing the focus away from titles and power, and getting people to focus on their work *today,* you give them more chances to succeed.

Of course we rely heavily on positive reinforcement, both verbal and financial, such as spot bonuses when an employee brings in business. But these are rewards that people can reach every day at work if they want, rather than work for years just to get that fancy title.

Shrink the Clock

At KTG we are always going a million miles an hour. And it is precisely this warp-speed mentality that creates Big Bangs. Great ideas almost always come when the deadline is careening into sight. Paul Zuckerman, the artistic director of *Chicago City Limits,* the New York City improv troupe, who also does management consulting on creativity, told me that "ideas don't come slowly. I've been on a lot of panels with creative people, and I've seen that with a number of plays or TV shows, the original idea exploded overnight."

A Big Bang is most likely to happen at the last possible moment, so it's crucial to maintain the sense that time is running out.

Those of us who went to business school were taught to spend a lot of time analyzing and rationalizing. We learned that good decisions are made from prudent consideration. Not in marketing. Marketing ideas are like fish. They don't improve with time. Many businesses, however, don't realize this. They simply suffer from inertia. Meetings to schedule meetings. Five layers of approval. Strategies to develop strategies. It is a miracle that any idea can survive in these environments. What may start out as innovative withers on the vine as it gets analyzed and refined.

If you maintain the sense that there is never a moment to waste, you will end up with a group of people who are constantly ready to create, who are on the alert, and, above all, who are *paying attention*. Attention is what it's all about, according to Mihaly Csikszentmihalyi, author of the best-selling *Flow: The Psychology of Optimal Experience*. "Because attention determines what will or will not appear in consciousness," he writes, "and because it is also required to make any other mental events—such as remembering, thinking, feeling, and making decisions—happen there, it is useful to think of it as psychic energy. Attention is like energy in that without it no work can be done, and in doing work it is dissipated."

And nothing gets people's attention more than fear that someone else will get the gig if you don't act instantly. It's like that stereotypical sci-fi movie scene when asteroids are flying at you a zillion miles an hour and the adrenaline kicks in and suddenly you save everyone's life. People are at their best when they sense that time's up.

Sandy Beall, chairman and CEO of Ruby Tuesday, owes the success of the restaurant chain to the ability of the company to move quickly. "We are more ready-fire-aim than most organizations. We run our business basically on a weekly basis. We constantly throw out ideas and make decisions that can have high impact. We execute on a rapid-fire basis. Some people overthink and overanalyze things to death and opportunity passes them." And it's worked. The company started in 1972 with one restaurant, and now owns 650 restaurants all over the world.

In the mid-1980s, when the animation department at Disney was floundering, says Joe Flower in *Prince of the Magic Kingdom: Michael Eisner and the Re-Making of Disney,* Eisner set up a "gong show" meeting on a Saturday morning when everyone had to enter the room with five ideas. "The format had become the favored means to jumpstart a division or project that needed new life," says Flower. "If the Disney animation department were to survive, it would need a lot of ideas that had box-office potential." At the end of the meeting, Eisner and his deputy, Jeff Katzenberg, left with an armful of ideas, including one that was inspired by a Hans Christian Andersen fairy tale. Ordinarily, the following approval process took weeks, even months, says Flower, but by Monday the animators got the green light for the fairy tale—and soon children across the country were watching *The Little Mermaid*.

Another example of the power of inspiration under pressure was recently recounted to me by Phil Dusenberry, retired chairman of BBDO North America. Years ago he was pitching the GE business. At the time, GE employed several major agencies to work on various product lines, and they had decided to consolidate all their accounts into one agency. So they asked each of their agencies to compete for the winner-takes-all account. "The night before the presentation, we had everything in place," remembers Dusenberry. "We had the commercials, the storyboards, the music. We had everything except one detail. The theme line of the campaign. Someone had written a clunky line, 'We make the things that make life good,' which sounded more like a line out of a memo than for an ad.

"So I went home and sat up until two o'clock in the morning until I finally wrote the line that I felt could become the theme line for the campaign."

The next morning, CEO Jack Welch walked into a room filled with three giant screens emblazoned with the words "We bring good things to life."

"The minute he saw it, we knew he loved it and we knew that we would get the account," says Dusenberry. Indeed, two days later he got the phone call that he had won the business. The theme line became GE's mantra, and ran for nearly two decades.

In today's marketplace the difference between Big Bang and Big Bust can often be counted in days, as the story of Continental Airlines' amazing turnaround reveals. In 1994, the company was about to declare bankruptcy for the *third time* when Gordon Bethune took over. In his book *From Worst to First,* which provides a behind-the-scenes look at the company's remarkable comeback, Bethune describes how Continental was a horrible place to work and a horrible airline to fly. The company was consistently ranked on the bottom of every list. Employees like baggage handlers and mechanics who had the Continental badge on their shirts would rip the label off, so when they stopped at Wal-Mart on the way home from work, no one would know they worked at Continental.

When Bethune took the reins, he could have put in place a grand five-year plan to overhaul the company. Instead, he focused on problems he could fix in sixty days: Get the planes there on time. Stop flying money-losing routes. ("Why are we flying six times a day from Greensboro, North Carolina, to Greenville, South Carolina?" he once famously said. "Who has a girlfriend there?")

One of his first directives was to require that all planes look alike. This was no small feat: The company started out as a bunch of small airlines like People's Express that were grouped together under the Continental umbrella. Very few of the planes looked alike. And remaking a plane is extremely costly, not just because of the work involved, but also because of the lost revenue when the plane is out of service. This was beside the point, Bethune said, and demanded that all planes be repainted in *sixty days*. Needless to say, they were, and Continental went on to become one of the most famous turnarounds in airline history.

The bottom line is this: *Time doesn't help*. When a deadline is in the distant future, we all can find a million other things to do. At KTG, we assume the deadline is *now*. When someone's stuck on an idea, we all stop what we're doing and start brainstorming until the crisis is over. We figure, what the hell, we're all here, let's just solve this. When you have to make decisions in a short period of time, you screen out everything else except that one thing. In the intense pressure of the moment, you really focus, and suddenly you have a million ideas. Just remember all those term papers you were miraculously able to write the night before they were due.

We attempt to create a pressure cooker environment at our company by demanding instant solutions. If you give people lots of time, you end up with lots of inhibitions watering down their great ideas. Instead, put people on the spot so they don't have time to edit their thoughts. Harvard Business School professor Teresa Amabile studied creativity and innovation in team environments and reported in *Harvard Management Update* that "when a team member does not have enough work or deadlines to work against, you may not get her best ideas, highest levels of motivation, or even her attention."

Phil Lee, a New York sports psychiatrist and coauthor of *Shrink Your Handicap: A Revolutionary Program from an Acclaimed Psychiatrist and a Top 100 Golf Instructor,* points out that athletes who hesitate play with fire: "They say that golf is a mental game. And they are right. In perhaps no other sport can your mental state

Go on an Email Diet

Email is one of the biggest time wasters in corporate life. What was once accomplished in a simple quick meeting often takes days of email exchanges to resolve. Robin, Gerry, Lisa, and I once had a day-and-a-half email exchange about which Fridays the staff could take off in the summer. The time we spent on the email exchange probably equaled one of those days off! Don't copy half the company phone book with your message just to cover your derriere. Eliminate the Emily Post replies—"Thanks!" or "Great job!" or "Good idea!"—and limit yourself to emails that move things forward.

wreak such havoc upon your physical performance. The overriding reason for this is time—the extraordinary amount of dead time between shots. In a four-hour round there is at most four minutes of hitting the ball. The remaining three hours and fifty-six minutes is a petri dish for growing doubt and anxiety. It's hard to play any sport well when there is too much time to think.

"In nonsporting endeavors too much time can be equally disadvantageous. Everyone knows that in taking the college boards it is wise to go with your first answer unless you have a very good reason for changing it. Too much time to think can here also lead to second guessing and poor performance."

One way to get people moving is to create false deadlines. Last year, working on the Panasonic men's shaver account, we were planning to shoot a man-on-the-street ad, where our actor would interview guys walking by. It was scheduled to take three, possibly four days. On the first day, our crew was relaxed as they headed out the door, viewing the day ahead as the warm-up day.

No such luck. I stopped them and said, "I want you to change your whole mind-set. I want you to pretend that today is the only day for the shoot. I want you to come back at end of the day with your commercial completely done. I want you to show me something that's brilliant."

At first everyone looked at me and said, "You don't understand, we have four days to lock this up," and I said, "No, *you* don't understand. You're gonna get that spot today, you're gonna have a finished commercial, and the rest is going to be gravy." Jolted into action, the crew went out and got terrific footage—the best of the four days.

Another way to keep things moving is to run your meetings like an improv session. In improv there's an exercise called "Yes, and," when you have to respond as if everything your partner says is true, even if it's not. There is no time to think about what the response should be. There is literally no time to ponder. You just react.

Saying yes keeps the discussion alive, says Keith Johnstone, in *Improv: Improvisation and the Theatre*. "Those who say 'Yes' are rewarded by the adventures they have," Johnstone points out, "and those who say 'No' are rewarded by the safety they attain. There are far more 'No' sayers around than 'Yes' sayers, but you can train one type to behave like the other." If you answer a suggestion with "No," you risk humiliating your staff, which is a sure creativity killer. A positive response, on the other hand, keeps everyone moving full speed ahead.

One technique that usually succeeds in getting great ideas on the table is to instill a certain amount of anxiety in people to get them revved up. Five days before an important meeting with a prospective client, I'll convene the staff and say, "We've got nothing. It's terrible, it's horrible. We don't have it." It's an exercise that makes people nervous, but often that nervous energy is exactly what inspires good thinking. Think back to the frantic moment when NASA engineers were told to create a carbon dioxide filter for the *Apollo 13* astronauts stranded in space. They were given all the contents of the astronauts' space capsule and told to improvise a new filter in mere hours. And they did. The brokerage Cantor Fitzgerald, one of the primary victims of the World Trade Center terrorist attack, is another example. By September 13 the firm was back in business, despite having lost over half of its employees.

In the mid-1980s I was a creative director on the Burger King account for J. Walter Thompson. We were running a campaign called "The Battle of the Burgers," which pitted our flame-broiled Whopper against McDonald's Big Mac for taste appeal. The Whopper overwhelmingly won in taste tests and our campaign helped to kick some of the sesame seeds off Big Mac buns. We were set to produce a number of commercials and were in the midst of casting them, when Rob Snyder, my art director, and our producer, Pam Maythenyi, called me. They told me that they had just discovered a little four-year-old girl who was too funny for words, and that we had to write a spot for her.

I didn't have a clue how a four-year-old could even *eat* a Whopper, never mind do a testimonial for one, but once I saw the casting tape I just knew we had to use her. A mass of brown curls framing an adorable dimpled face, and a stage presence that would have put Ethel Merman to shame. I quickly took the next plane out to Los Angeles from New York and somewhere over Iowa, I cowrote the spot with Rob's partner, Alan Braunstein.

Later, somewhere over Nevada, we read the script to Greg Weinschenker, my partner, and the next day we shot a totally hilarious commercial called "Tea Party," superbly directed by Weinschenker. Within 24 hours of seeing this little girl, we ended up shooting a commercial that won the Clio that year for best performance by a child.

Another trick that we use to keep things moving quickly is to compress as many meetings as possible into one. Too many times in business people set up meetings to decide what the next meeting should be about. And everyone else is only too happy to follow suit. Yet at most meetings, everyone is trying to think of the fastest way to get out of the room. If you say, "OK, I'll be back in a week with the proposal," that gets you out of the room. Unfortunately, it also means nothing will happen today.

Instead, the best way to have a good first meeting is to anticipate the second meeting and have that one instead. If I read a script and decide that it needs a funny ending, I don't convene the troops to say, Here's what you need to do, and then send them off to their offices. Instead, we sit there until we come up with an ending that cracks up everyone in the room.

This happens over and over with our presentations. Traditionally in advertising when you are competing for a particular account, you meet with the prospective client at least twice. First you pitch your strategy and company, introducing the client to your way of doing business. The client could see as many as two dozen agencies, then he or she will cull through the contenders and come up with a list of finalists. It is only at this point, if you get a call-back, that you have the "creative" meeting when you present your ad campaign, your ideas for various commercials.

In the spring of 2001 we were invited to be the finalists for the Coldwell Banker Real Estate Corporation pitch. They were accustomed to getting all their ducks in a row, even going to the lengths of faxing out a series of questions to all the finalists. This, they figured, would help them narrow down the list.

Well, we never got around to that list of questions. While working on a strategy for the client, we thought that we could wow them if we also had a specific idea for an ad campaign. A few days before we were to see them, we came up with something hilarious and just perfect for this upscale realtor. The day of the meeting, despite the fact that we knew it was not supposed to include creative work, we presented our ad campaign anyway. It was an idea that featured realtors dancing the tango with their clients, illustrating the concept that Coldwell Banker is your "perfect partner." We circumvented the process, the client just couldn't get our tango jingle out of his head, and a few weeks later we won the account.

The campaign increased the brand awareness among consumers nearly 35 percent.

Compressing your staff, time, and space establishes the perfect staging ground for Big Bangs. But how do you organize the creative process itself?

Well, you start by becoming *disorganized* . . .

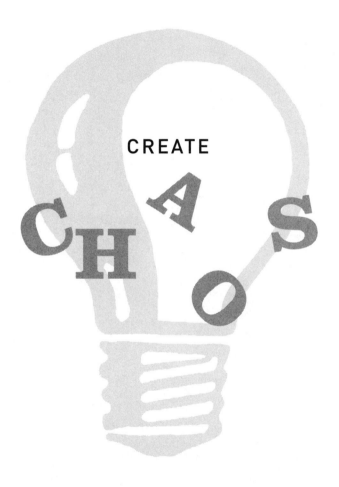

CREATE CHAOS

The one thing you can't order from Amazon.com is a great idea. Yet it's the most valuable commodity in marketing. But how do you prime people to come up with good ideas? How do you stop them from traveling down the same old paths, and think up something new?

The answer, we've found, is to embrace chaos. Why? Because creativity isn't logical. William James, in the 1880s, described creativity as "a seething cauldron of ideas, where everything is fizzling and bobbling about in a state of bewildering activity, where partnerships can be joined or loosened in an instant, treadmill routine is unknown, and the unexpected seems only law." In order to unlock the creative potential of everyone in your company, you need to allow a certain amount of disorganization.

A nonlinear way of thinking is crucial for today's constantly changing world, points out Irene Sanders, executive director of the Washington Center for Complexity and Public Policy. We can't even predict the weather accurately, much less human behavior. As a result, whether it's in business or in government, she argues, chaos allows us to look beyond simple cause-and-effect relationships to focus on more intuitive, associative thinking. In a recent article on the war on terrorism for the *Washington Post,* Sanders warns against underestimating the complexity of our world today: "For far too long, our military and intelligence establishments have simply analyzed the past in order to anticipate the future—relying on what's commonly called a linear way of thinking. When you think you have all the answers, you don't continue to ask questions." This is one of the reasons, Sanders argues, that our government failed to prevent the September 11 attacks.

In marketing, nonlinear thinking is the only way to catch the attention of today's continually evolving consumer. And nonlinear thinking can only happen in the right environment. We've had several instances where someone has come to work with us after a lackluster career elsewhere and is suddenly turning out hit after hit. In our informal, relaxed offices, creative people know that they are in a place where everything is up for grabs, no avenue is off limits, everything is a possibility. In the 1980s, IBM CEO John Akers failed in large part because of the stultifying atmosphere. He "believed in continuity, in gradual, incremental change," say Foster and Kaplan in *Creative Destruction,* yet "the world Akers and IBM knew was shifting under their feet as the dominance of the mainframe computer faded." The company, which heretofore thrived on organization, just couldn't handle the chaos brought to the industry by computer geeks tinkering in garages.

Even the most creative person in the world can be stymied by a buttoned-up atmosphere. Says New York psychologist Dr. Ona Robinson, "One of the problems that creative people have is that they often don't bring things to closure. This is because they can entertain many possibilities all at the same time." It's similar to quantum theory, where every single possible permutation of an event is possible until it actually occurs—at which point only one permutation is possible and all other possibilities are closed off.

A Big Bang company must maintain an atmosphere of perpetual possibilities for as long as possible. Eventually, of course, decisions have to be made, but too many organizations end the discussion early in order to be efficient—and end up losing to competitors who can withstand the chaos of nonlinear thinking.

Embracing chaos means that you accept the fact that great, mammoth, earth-shattering ideas can often come from really boring, seemingly random ones. Mihaly Czikszentmihalyi, psychologist and author of *Flow,* reminds us that "Archimedes was not the first to have seen a bathtub overflow, Newton the falling of an apple, or Watt the steam escaping from a teapot, but these three did notice the broader implications of these trivial, almost everyday occurrences."

Here's a recent KTG success story that started from a trivial thought, indeed.

Milk It

In the fall of 2000 KTG won a project from Parmalat milk. We were thrilled to get the business, but now we had to come up with an idea for their new vitamin E–enriched skim milk. As usual, the day before we were supposed to present some terrific campaign for the Parmalat folks, we didn't have one idea that clicked.

It was 10 P.M., and about eight creative people were crammed into my office. The client had given us a stack of papers about the benefits of vitamin E, how it helps the skin stay vibrant and clear, and how it's good for your overall health. We spent a lot of time fruitlessly trying to come up with something along these lines. It was incredibly frustrating. At one low point, we actually spent a good five minutes trying to find a word that rhymed with "epidermis." This is getting us nowhere, I thought to myself, and started to talk about my earliest memories of milk.

Someone else started to talk about being lactose intolerant. Another person said he still drinks a lot of milk. Soon everyone was chiming in with childhood reminiscences.

Most bosses at this point would have rebuked the staff and forced everyone back to the issue at hand. But I have learned that creative minds need just this kind of meandering to allow creativity to catch fire. So I let the conversation just wander.

"I used to think chocolate milk came from chocolate cows," said Gerry Killeen, our managing director of creative services, laughing.

"I love the taste of skim milk," I interjected at one point.

"How could you possibly like skim milk?" Robin Schwarz, one of our writers, blurted out. "It tastes horrible! It's like white water!"

"Well I started drinking it when I was a kid, so I guess I got used to it."

"When I was a kid," Robin answered, "I didn't even know what skim milk was. I didn't understand the word 'skim,' so I just thought everyone was calling it 'skin milk.'"

Well, we all stopped talking and suddenly realized, Eureka! Skin Milk was the *perfect* way to describe this Vitamin E–enriched product. And from there we created the ad: First you see a closeup of a beautiful white creamy substance swirling around in a jar. As the announcer talks about this wonderful new skin product, enriched with vitamin E, you think you're watching a commercial for face crème. Then the camera pulls back and you see a woman put her hand around the jar and drink it. The announcer says, "It's Parmalat vitamin E–enriched skim milk, but we like to call it Skin Milk." When we showed it to the Parmalat folks the next afternoon, they loved it.

Now, all that rambling and tangential discussion at 10 P.M. the night before an important meeting may seem very inefficient. But by allowing people to be intuitive instead of forcing them to stay on topic, interesting connections are made, and great ideas bubble up to the surface. Creativity expert Roger von Oech points out that Renaissance kings had a court jester on hand just to shake things up: "It was the fool's job to parody any proposal under discussion to make it appear in a fresh light. He might extol the trivial, trifle the exalted, or reverse the common perception of a situation. Example: 'If a man is sitting backward on a horse, why do we assume that it is the man who is backward and not the horse?' Result: He dislodged people's assumptions and allowed them to see things in a fresh light."

A Big Bang company allows people to put existing elements together in an unconventional way, to think laterally instead of

THIS CLEVER NAME FOR A VITAMIN E–ENRICHED MILK WAS SKIMMED FROM A TOTALLY IMPROMPTU CONVERSATION.

linearly. We call this the chaos theory of creativity, and below we discuss how we encourage chaos in our company.

Stop Being So Polite

Many corporate bosses spend an inordinate amount of time making sure that everything's proper. Flow charts dictate the progress of each project. Criticism is handled delicately. A certain etiquette is demanded around the office, where everyone is polite, no one raises his voice, and silliness can render you promotion-proof. It's almost as if they put up a pretend sign that says, "Ahem, we're doing business now, we don't sing songs or talk about our personal lives. We pass out lots of reading material and look at charts." How much time we waste fitting our work into a preset business-like box!

Few people come up with brilliant, disruptive ideas in an atmosphere like this. Of course there's a time and a place for business-like demeanors, but if you spend all your time worrying about proper work flow and social etiquette, you'll stifle the free flow of ideas. In the long run, it's much more productive to *minimize* order.

In its early days, 3M was a classic example of a company that benefitted from an atmosphere of loosely defined boundaries. The result was a long list of Big Bangs. In the early 1920s, the company's primary product was still sandpaper, yet that didn't stop an employee who happened to be at an auto-body shop one day. He overheard a paint man swearing because he couldn't paint two-tone cars (very trendy at the time) without leaving blotches and wavy lines. The 3M employee went back to his office and invented masking tape—despite the fact that he had no formal orders to solve such a problem. This discovery eventually led to Scotch tape, and, ultimately, Post-its. As Collins and Porras note in *Built to Last,* "Although the invention of the Post-it note might have been somewhat accidental, the creation of the 3M environment that allowed it was anything but an accident."

You have to set up an environment that allows the synapses to connect in unexpected ways. And to do that, you have to get people to loosen up their minds and let down their defenses. Brilliance and creativity require minds uncluttered with petty worries about whether they said the right thing. People who are relaxed are more creative and more willing to say whatever comes to mind.

One of the best ways to encourage informality is to simply wander around. In *Lincoln on Leadership: Executive Strategies for Tough Times,* author Donald T. Phillips recounts how the president would spend most of his day wandering in and out of cabinet members' offices, striking up casual conversations, or bursting in on meetings to have a quick chat. "For Lincoln," Phillips writes, "casual contact with his subordinates was as important as formal gatherings, if not more so . . . He preferred, whenever possible, to interact with people when they were in a more relaxed, less pressure-packed environment."

This "Theory of Wandering Around" encourages people to get

Put Up with the Mess

Messy offices are often the sign of percolating ideas. Old documents, videotapes, and storyboards that pile up on windowsills may just need a little time to age in the sunlight. Then, during an enforced semiannual clean-up (say, when the window washers appear), that half-finished draft can shed light on a current project. At KTG, we have found this cycle of collecting and enforced sifting to be a good creative spark plug—so we happily put up with the disarray in certain corners. Occasionally, an idea that didn't fly with one client turns out to be the perfect solution for another.

out of their offices or outposts and mingle with their colleagues. We often discuss ideas with small ad hoc groups in the hallway or have impromptu meetings with whomever is around. It's important that people feel uninhibited, and free to walk into each other's personal space.

P&G exec Ravi Chaturvedi spends a good part of his day wandering around his offices. "There is no question that you pick up a lot by just walking around and saying, 'What are you working on and how can I help?'" he says. Instead of scheduling formal meetings when people are supposed to present finished ideas, Chaturvedi has weekly meetings where there is an open agenda and people can bring up any issue. "I don't ever set the agenda, or the only time these guys see me is when it's with a recommendation for me to say 'yes' or 'no.' Also, I have a 'Fireside Chat' every month and people can simply talk to me about what's on their mind. It's not being set up as a 'yes' or 'no' meeting."

At KTG, I encourage people to wander into my office whenever they think they're on to something. Two minds are (almost) always better than one. That's when sparks start to fly. A perfect example of this occurred in the late 1990s, when we were working on the campaign for the American Red Cross. We were looking for something that would tap into all the millennium fever. Copywriter Robin Schwarz marched unannounced into my office one morning and said, "I've got it. You see this baby and the announcer says, 'When this baby is 8 there is going to be a terrible fire and the Red Cross will save her house. When this baby is 21, she will have an accident and the Red Cross will provide blood. Then she's going to have a child, and there will be a terrible tornado, and the Red Cross will rebuild the town.' "

"C'mon, Robin," I said, dropping what I was doing. "Who is the Red Cross—God? How would they know all this? How would they know what was going to happen—wait! *What if we turn this whole thing around?*"

We worked together for another ten minutes and came up with

a script that the American Red Cross loved: "A new century is coming. And with it, a thousand questions. Will there be peace? Will your family ever be in harm's way? Will a small town in Texas be hit with a hurricane? Will your daughter ever need a new kind of blood transfusion? Will that nice man who hands you the paper ever need a hand to hold in a time of need? We've got no crystal ball. Just one promise. We'll be there."

Even though her original idea was rough and hadn't yet been perfected, Robin felt comfortable just barging in on me. While many employees feel compelled to present only perfect work to their bosses, people at KTG know we often get great ideas from half-baked ones as well.

Finally, we encourage a footloose atmosphere at KTG by tolerating behavior that wouldn't fly in most nursery schools. We let emotions run high. In many corporate cultures, open argument and confrontation are absolutely not tolerated. We believe this just results in a lot of negative passive-aggressive behavior. Instead, we allow heated arguments and direct criticism (provided no one says anything personally offensive).

We also tolerate wacky humor that would get chastised elsewhere. Laughing frees everybody up. Freud, in his book *Jokes and Their Relation to the Unconscious* (Freud wasn't much of a cut-up when it came to book titles), wrote that the essence of humor lies in one's ability to draw similarities between disparate thoughts and ideas. Watching a refined gentleman slipping on a banana peel creates laughter, while a monkey slipping on a banana peel just looks like he dropped his lunch. Joke-telling helps everyone make the kind of disparate connections that can lead to brilliant ideas.

Let Employees Find Their Niche

It doesn't take a Mensa member to realize that people do their best work when they are doing what they do best. After I decided to start a company, I called a handful of people to come on board.

Among the first to say yes (besides, naturally, Robin) was Gerry Killeen, a friend with whom I'd worked for years. I remembered that along with being a gifted copywriter, Gerry has the ability to organize and motivate creative people. The downfall of most startup agencies is not a lack of ideas, but the inability to simply get the work done, to see that people are using their time well, and to make sure the storyboards are actually in the portfolio before you leave for the airport. We needed someone who could do all that.

I had no job description at all when I offered Gerry a job. During the interview, she asked me what she would be doing. I said, "I don't know, but I do know that you'll be very, very busy." Today, Gerry is the Managing Director, Creative Services, organizing not only the creative work flow at KTG, but also spearheading many of its internal operations. She's also very good at coming up with one-line zingers, so she's often in creative meetings. Had she been adept at heart surgery, however, our agency would today be competing with Cedars-Sinai for patients.

When we hire someone, we deliberately start out by saying, "Yes, we want to hire you because we think you are very talented and very bright." And then we tell the person to create his job. Of course we always have a loose job description in mind, but it works out much better if the person can suss out where she or he best fits in. As Gerry notes, "When a person knows that he or she is limited only by imagination—and not by the job description—it creates an electric, positively charged atmosphere that benefits everyone."

We have assistants who find music for creative presentations, account people who go to production sessions, art directors who write videos. Not so long ago we asked David Mester, a film editor at New York City–based Blue Rock Editing Company, to help us refine the videos that KTG uses for presentations. It became apparent early on, however, that Mester is much more than an editor. He turned out to be a great writer and performer. We started to ask him to do all our "brand" videos—clips that introduce KTG to prospective clients—and to help set up presentations at meetings.

Kill the Lights

The buzzing, cold green glow of standard-issue fluorescent lights "can be an obstacle that prevents the flow of creativity," says Angela Casola, a health psychologist based in Denver, Colorado. Of course it's an expensive proposition to revamp the lighting in your entire office, but there's a cheaper way. In the early days of KTG, when we started to notice that people would rather sit in virtual darkness than switch on their overhead lights, we made a trip to IKEA. With a fifteen-dollar-per-employee investment, everyone now happily works under the warm glow of indirect, incandescent lighting.

If we had erected strict barriers between departments, however, we never would have discovered what a great asset this guy is.

When you let people wander into other territories, you get another benefit: a new perspective. Successful companies have built this idea into businesses, by assigning a certain number of production managers to move from team to team to cross-pollinate their laboratories, according to Collins and Porras in *Built to Last*.

In a client-oriented business, of course, this concept can be a tough sell. Most clients prefer a traditional relationship where account management people are assigned to one account at a time for years. It seems more organized that way. The result, however, is that many folks in our business can quickly become pigeonholed into working on the same things over and over again. They know everything there is to know about a category like Frozen Novelty Treats (think Dove Bars) and little else. Until ultimately, you have someone who hasn't had a new idea in years and has put on twenty-five pounds to boot!

We usually discourage this arrangement. Yes, clients take on risk when they entrust confidential business information to more than one person. But, in turn, they get intellectually stimulated people who love their jobs. Clients are much more likely to get a Big Bang if an account person has the opportunity to work on many pieces of business at the same time. Foster and Kaplan, in *Creative Destruction,* note that working on many things at once "is a common pattern among creative individuals; it keeps them from getting bored or stymied, and it produces an unexpected cross-fertilization of ideas."

Look for Ideas in Unlikely Places

Big Bangs can come at any time, in any place, but you have to be open to seeing them. You can't get hung up on what should or shouldn't be. Consider the following unlikely ideas, hardly the result of one-track minds. Navy researchers, trying to develop a more flexible robotic arm, studied octopuses. Rutgers University mathematicians looking for inventive problem-solving techniques turned to origami. Big Bang ideas are usually the result of making a curious or circuitous connection that no one else has made before.

There is a tenet of chaos theory, called *the butterfly principle,* that claims that every single event, no matter how small, has a ripple effect that can be enormous. In his book *Does God Play Dice? The Mathematics of Chaos,* Ian Stewart explains it this way: "The flapping of a single butterfly's wing today produces a tiny change in the state of the atmosphere. Over a period of time, what the atmosphere actually does diverges from what it would have done. So, in a month's time, a tornado that would have devastated the Indonesian coast doesn't happen. Or maybe one that wasn't going to happen, does."

In other words, seemingly inconsequential things can start a chain reaction to something huge. A thought, word, or idea from some realm of life can influence thinking about a current project.

When Chris Clouser was vice president of corporate relations

Break One Habit Each Day

In order to come up with disruptive ideas, you need to train your brain to connect in unusual and twisted ways. In *Keep Your Brain Alive,* by Manning Rubin and Lawrence C. Katz, Ph.D., the authors explain that using your five senses in unexpected ways can increase creativity. They offer several suggestions: Bring five different doughnuts to work and, when the urge strikes, identify them using only your sense of smell and taste. Choose a different route to work today. Eat only red-colored foods for lunch. The point isn't what habits you break, but rather that you get in the habit of breaking habits.

and advertising for Bell Atlantic in the 1980s, he was struggling to find a way to promote the newly formed company. Bell Atlantic was a conglomerate of Baby Bells, such as Bell of New Jersey and Bell of Pennsylvania, and he was trying to come up with a way to warm up the company's image. It was at a time when consumers would open their phone bill and see a new company name and wonder, who is this? Instead of just being a public utility, he wanted to have the company play a role in the lives of its consumers.

One night at home, thinking of nothing in particular, he was watching the news and heard that there was going to be a low voter turnout for the upcoming Reagan/Dukakis election. Suddenly he realized that this could be the hook he was looking for.

He got in touch with several lawmakers from each party and got them to agree to appear in get-out-the-vote commercials sponsored by Bell Atlantic. Presidents Ford and Carter both appeared in a commercial that ended with Bell Atlantic's tagline, "We're more than just talk." The commercial was so good that it got "road-blocked"—shown on every major network at the same time—during the evening news just days before the election. It was the perfect way for his company to tell its consumers that they were more than just a faceless entity that sends you a bill each month. If Clouser didn't have the ability to see ideas anywhere, at any time, the commercial, written by the talented Bill Lane, never would have happened.

Cheryl Berman, chief creative officer of Leo Burnett USA, has a similar story. She was working on the United Airlines account a few years ago and was flying in one of its planes to Hawaii for a meeting. She noticed a flight attendant telling stories to a group of passengers about his native Hawaii. He talked about his Hawaiian grandmother, about the welcoming nature of Hawaiians and how the people are gentle and friendly. "I looked around and saw everyone on the plane mesmerized by this guy, so I thought if it can work here, it can work in a commercial," remembers Berman. On the spot, she got the guy's name and took notes about his story. Soon after, the flight attendant was starring in a commercial for United Airlines.

This same marketing butterfly principle led to a recent KTG Big Bang.

The Skinny on Blimpie

In May of 2002 we were asked to compete for the Blimpie account. We came up with a very disruptive idea simply because I decided to take my daughter, Emily, out one night.

We went to a comedy club where kids get up and tell jokes to each other. One kid did a whole routine on Jared from the Subway commercial. For the uninitiated, Subway was running a series of commercials featuring a real guy named Jared who claims he lost over 200 pounds by eating Subway's healthy sandwiches.

Blimpie, by the time they contacted KTG, was just furious that Subway was so successful with these ads. During the previous five years, Blimpie's market share was shrinking, while Subway's increased from 27 to 30 percent. Blimpie couldn't get angry enough that they were losing their lunch to Subway.

I went in to work the next day and said, "You know what? That Jared guy is a Big Bang. Everybody thinks that Subway is this really healthy place because you can eat but still lose weight. We've got to do something with Jared. We need to write a spot making fun of him. It might not end up being the final campaign, but it could get Blimpie's attention." Then I wrote a spot where Jared lost weight because every time he looked at one of those Subway sandwiches he puked.

But even I draw the line at prime-time puking. So I called my staff in, read them my script, and said, "We can't legally use Jared for a commercial, but maybe there's something in this idea of getting thin because the food doesn't seem appealing."

One of our teams, copywriter Andy Landorf and art director Whitney Pillsbury, went off to one of the conference rooms to hash out some ideas. At one point, Andy, imitating Jared's smug tones, said, "I'm so skinny because I diet—wait a minute, I've got it! I'm so skinny because I eat nothing at all! I don't even eat!"

"You're as skinny as a rail—" returned Whitney.

"As skinny as a fencepost!"

"As a—a—hold on!" said Whitney excitedly as he ran out of the room. He tore open the cleaning closet door, grabbed a floor mop, and came back. He hid behind the conference room door, stuck the mop out, swishing the top as if it were blond tresses, and started screeching, "Hi! Hi! Look at me! I'm so *skinny!*"

Andy jumped in, "You know why I'm so skinny?? I'm on that Subway diet! I go there for lunch and the food is so bad that *I don't eat!*"

And so the "Mop" ad for Blimpie was created:

Guy walking down the street sees an upside-down
mop bouncing merrily along, her ropy tresses
swinging.

> *Guy:* Ellen?? You look so—so skinny!
>
> *Mop:* Well, you know that commercial where the guy loses weight and he eats subs?
>
> *Guy:* Yeah.
>
> *Mop:* Well, I'm on that diet!
>
> *Guy:* But they use presliced deli meat. How can you eat that stuff?
>
> *Mop:* I *don't!* That's why I'm so *skinny!* . . . [lowers her voice] Can I ask you a question? Do I look fat?

The Blimpie account people nearly fell off their chairs laughing at the ad, and it won us a $15 million piece of business. Two months later the ad ran on *Saturday Night Live, Frasier,* and *NYPD Blue.* And it prompted a column in the *Wall Street Journal.*

GETTING THE "SKINNY" ON BLIMPIE'S FRESH-SLICED DELI MEAT.

The development of this ad is a perfect example of the butterfly principle: I take my kid out, hear a joke about Jared, and come back to the office, and tell my staff to make fun of this guy. Whitney and Andy are assigned to the account, they walk by the cleaning closet on the way to the conference room . . . and a great idea results. As T. Irene Sanders notes, consumer behavior is a complex system, and this kind of nonlinear thinking is the only way "to create opportunities, create marketing approaches to tap into changing patterns or emotions that really capture people's attention."

In order to get people to see ideas in unlikely places, you need to encourage them to entertain every possibility. When you're walking down the street, you need to say to yourself, How can I tie that to what I'm doing? This is where many Big Bang ideas come from.

This is exactly how I came up with a concept for a children's PBS series. My son Michael is a chess prodigy and was the subject of a book, *The Making of a Chess Champion,* by Barry Berg. The book, a staple in many elementary school libraries, has encouraged children across the nation to pursue chess, despite its difficulty. When I realized just how powerful the book was, I went to PBS to suggest a show called *Amazing Kids.* The concept was a series that would celebrate kids who are truly remarkable in various arenas: skating, for example, or standup comedy. I imagined a totally interactive show, with the kids available for on-line chats or advice, a show that would ultimately celebrate the potential of all children to realize their dreams. PBS loved it, and hopes to make it available to parents and children throughout America. This potential Big Bang came about simply because of a random thought one day while I was looking at the book about my son.

Another random connection led to one of America's most recognized icons: the Campbell's soup can. In 1898, Herberton Williams, one of the company's top brass, attended a football game between rival Ivy Leaguers Cornell and University of Pennsylvania. Struck by the brilliant red-and-white uniforms sported by the Cornell team, Williams had an inspiration right there in the bleachers. What if the company used this eye-catching color combination for its logo? He convinced the company to make the switch, and the rest is pop history.

One of my first Big Bangs came about in a similar fashion, when I was having a quick dinner with some friends.

A Sandwich on the Run

In the early 1980s, when I was a copywriter for J. Walter Thompson, I was asked to help come up with some ads for French's mustard. Mustard isn't exactly a spicy topic for anybody, so I was desperate for ideas. One night I went out to dinner with a friend, Laurie Garnier, a sensational writer and now the global creative director on KTG's Clairol account. As I started to put mustard on my pastrami sandwich, I suddenly said to her, "Wouldn't it be funny if I didn't put French's mustard on this sandwich, but some other brand, and it got mad and started running away?" Laurie looked me squarely in the face and said, "That's ridiculous," and we went on to gossip about other things. But that got me thinking.

The next morning I went in to James Patterson, my boss at the time and now the mega-best-selling novelist, and told him about my idea. Mind you, talking food was nearly unheard of at the time. He immediately saw that this execution had the power to disrupt. It was so cockeyed, he suspected, that it just might get people's attention. I was thrilled to hear that the client agreed. They bought it and the final spot ran as follows.

The ad starts out looking like a typical, boring food commercial, with a roast-beef sandwich waiting to be spread with mustard. A knife loaded with generic mustard hovers into view, heading for the sandwich. All of a sudden the sandwich shrinks back with a resounding shriek of horror. The same thing happens with a croissant-wich, and a pita sandwich, as a voiceover admonishes, "If you're not giving your sandwich French's mustard, it may not like it!" Then the sandwiches start running away from the knife because it's dripping with the wrong mustard. At the end of the ad, all the sandwiches

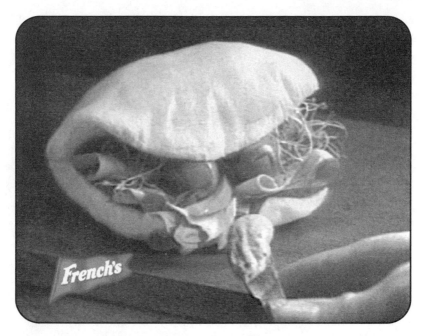

A SUSPICIOUS SANDWICH RECOILS FROM A RIVAL BRAND THAT JUST DOESN'T CUT THE MUSTARD.

started applauding when a knife slathered with French's mustard shows up, and a tagline written by Manning Rubin appears, "Be good to your food."

The ad was a phenomenal success on all counts. We won two Clios (the advertising industry's equivalent to Oscars) and an Effie (the marketing industry's equivalent). "And while the competition was spending easily ten times what we were spending," remembers Martin J. Rose, formerly the account director on French's, "this ad had the ability to break through the clutter and get recognition. We only had a budget of between $2 and $3 million, but it was really impactful creative stuff."

Don't get sucked into conventional ways that we filter out ideas. If your mind is open to any possibility, you're much likelier to end up with an idea that disrupts. I've learned this again and again. When I was at Wells, Rich, Greene, I once went into copywriter Steve Baer's office to see how he was doing on some work for

Heineken. I saw a drawing on his desk that had a sketch of the red Heineken star. Underneath the star were scribbled the words, "snappy headline goes here." At the bottom of the page were the words "logo here."

"How cool! What a great idea for an ad," I said.

"Well, actually, it isn't an ad, they're just instructions for the art director," said Steve.

"Let's use it!" I said.

"You mean this, just like this? You're kidding!"

"Why not! It's funny, and will get people's attention. It's totally disruptive because it breaks every rule about advertising. It's the last thing people expect."

Heineken loved the ad.

Improvisation is another way to mine ideas from unlikely places. Several lifetimes ago, I was one of five people in a New York City comedy troupe that used improv to come up with material. This experience taught me a lesson that I still use to this day: Improvisation leads to great ideas. Dr. Elspeth MacFadzean, a British researcher who focuses on creativity in the workplace, echoes this argument. She claims that "paradigm-breaking" requires the ability to bring "new elements into the problem" and to "break down perceptions and to completely smash the problem's boundaries." Often, she says, this requires using "unrelated stimuli and forced association," which is exactly what improvisation is all about.

"Improvisation is a way to tap into creativity," says Paul Zuckerman, artistic director of *Chicago City Limits*. "A lot of our training is counterintuitive to what people do. People always want to answer in the correct way. Ask people to think of a color. People have trouble. Why? They want to be right. 'If I say black, you'll think I'm depressed. If I say pink, you'll think I'm gay.' The improviser wants to rush right through whether or not it's right. As improvisers, we say, 'Forget about that stuff, forget about preconceptions.' You have to learn not to edit yourself. By staying in the moment, improvisation is a vehicle to readily access all that unfiltered stuff that's just under the surface. Just let yourself make intuitive connections. And that, ultimately, is what makes us funny."

Intuitive connections also lead to great ideas. The well-known brainstorming company, Synectics Corporation in Cambridge, Massachusetts, will ask clients to stop thinking about the problem at hand—say, a new way to market plastic baggies—and think about something else—say, Venetian blinds. Then, clients will be told to try to put the two disparate products together to come up with, say, a new way to seal baggies. Velcro came about in just such a way: When a Swiss engineer was hunched over a pair of pants covered with burrs, he suddenly wondered if Mother Nature had invented a better zipper. His hunch led to the 1952 opening of a company called Velcro (from the French "velour" for velvet and "crochet" for hook).

Encouraging people to say whatever comes to mind, however, is a counterintuitive concept in business. This is not easy for most executives to do. Zuckerman notes that the biggest block to improvising is the failure to listen. Ordinarily, when someone speaks to

Encourage Interruptions

In some offices, it is considered bad form to interrupt a meeting in progress. The person is expected to wait patiently outside your door or leave a message to get in touch when you are free. We welcome intruders into our conversations. Often, a person who is completely unaware of the problem at hand has a fresh solution, or even just a novel take on the issue. Leave doors open, or put up glass walls so that people won't feel intimidated about walking into a conversation in progress.

us we tune 50 percent of it out because we've already started thinking of a response. We're not really listening. The second you start screening out the other speaker, or thinking about what your next line is, you've tuned out the other person and lost the flow. In improv, you train yourself to listen and respond without forethought. "In a brainstorming session," says Zuckerman, "if someone brings up ideas that aren't in your mind-set, you almost can't wait until they shut up so you can bring your idea to the table." He recommends simply writing down your idea so that you can "forget about your idea and embrace the other person's. You can always go back to yours." That's why improvisors spend so much time on the yes-and theory. "I really encourage people to throw out good ideas and bad," says Zuckerman. "It sounds easy, but in fact we all have tremendous egos. The big breakthrough comes when you really can let go, and jump into someone else's idea."

Back Off

The marketing universe is filled with ideas yet to be hatched, products yet to be developed, solutions yet to be discovered. So naturally we spend most of our working hours in this vast developmental purgatory, anxiously waiting for the creative muse to catapult our thinking into one megamillion Big Bang. But when your focus and strategic thinking only succeed in sucking you further into the Black Hole of Mediocrity, you need to act on your most counterintuitive impulse: Do nothing.

What, you scream out, how could I do nothing? *Nothing* is what I have right now. *Nothing* is what I have to present to my client at tomorrow's meeting. *Nothing* is what our revenue will be if we don't come up with an idea. Yet when the brain is cluttered with fears, apprehensions, deadlines, and a thousand bad ideas, there's simply no room for the great one.

One of the first things we do at KTG when we hit a mental block is just walk away from it. Go into someone else's office, go home, or just take a walk. And like clockwork, suddenly the ideas begin ticking again. As Dr. Ona Robinson, a New York business psychologist tells it, "Removing yourself from your immediate surroundings gives the brain a breath of fresh, creative air. A new environment relaxes the synapses, as does even a change of body position, say, from sitting on a chair to maybe sitting on the floor. It tricks the mind into focusing on an outward change, which gives our gray matter a chance to recharge."

If there's time, sleep on it. Some of our greatest ideas flow out of REM sleep, when our subconscious goes to work and reaches from a wellspring of creative juices just waiting to be squeezed into our conscious thought. (The trick, of course, is to remember what the hell you dreamed, so always keep a pad nearby your pillow.) Bach, when talking about musical ideas, once said, "The problem is not finding them, it's—when getting up in the morning and getting out of bed—not stepping on them."

Encourage Failure

One of the biggest impediments to getting people to be creative is fear of failure. They just don't want to risk it, explains Jennifer Voigt Kaplan, an evolutionary psychologist from New Jersey. "It's difficult to spur creativity in organizations," says Kaplan, because "risk aversion is bred in our bones. Primitive human beings were not rewarded for taking extreme risks, because they did not survive as non–risk-takers did." This makes sense: When the very first person in Cave 20 offered to kill the woolly mammoth in heat, it was very likely that he wouldn't be joining his cavemates for dinner that night. Fortunately, modern penal codes prevent you from being slaughtered for coming up with a bad idea (unless you were the inventor of New Coke), but fear of risk is still with us today.

A talking duck. Prime-time orgasms. Pilot Pen envy. These are some pretty zany ideas. They easily could have been rejected outright. But we take every idea seriously, no matter how silly. Everyone must know that it's OK to come in with a really weird, unconventional—and perhaps really bad—idea. Says management consultant Sanders, "Creativity comes from your imagination. Creative people are intuitive, they have a wacky way of seeing connections, relationships, and underlying patterns and can't always explain how that happens." It comes back to the yes-and theory in improvisation, which assumes that no one is wrong, they are just halfway there. As James Joyce said, mistakes are "portals of discovery."

Creativity is not about safety; it is diametrically opposed to it. Some of the greatest works written by Beethoven, for instance, went against the conventions of his time. The string quartets that the great composer wrote at the end of his life, when he was completely deaf, are incredibly sophisticated, breaking free from nineteenth-century traditions and leaping ahead fifty or a hundred years. During Beethoven's time, however, few people would listen to them. One quartet ended with a movement so unorthodox that Beethoven decided to replace it with a finale more pleasing to nineteenth-century ears. The original finale, however, now known as the *Grosse Fuge*, is considered one of his most daring pieces. Indeed, Beethoven himself, when confronted with complaints that no one liked his *Grosse Fuge,* retorted, "They'll like it one day!"

If you want your staff to be courageous enough to come up with a disruptive Big Bang, you need to create an environment where risk-taking is safe—even encouraged. In a recent issue of *Organization Studies,* researchers Ken Kamoche and Miguel Pina e Cunha report that "in successful, highly innovative companies, mistakes are treated as an opportunity for organizational learning. . . . Failure resulting from risk-taking is rewarded . . . and managers accept and encourage 'rule-breaking.'" The key is to train yourself to be encouraging in the face of bad ideas, and to reward people for considering unusual, if unwise, courses of action. "You need to address what happens if you're creative and you fail," says evolutionary psychologist Kaplan. "You need to make failing safe. That's how you get people to think out of the box." Never punish or criticize bad ideas; instead, allow them to be part of the many possibilities that continue to exist until a single course of action is chosen. That bad idea can easily start a chain reaction to a good idea.

It takes practice to embrace Big Bang chaos. But just like a theatrical troupe, the members of your staff will get better and better at indulging their most creative selves as they work together. All they need now is to make contact with the lightning rod to the consumer's conscious mind: his heart.

It's no secret why sappy tearjerkers play in movie theaters to mass audiences, while documentaries air on PBS. As dozens of books on advertising reveal, emotion sells. An emotional pitch simplifies a message, allowing it to cut across economic, gender, or cultural lines. It's a basic concept. So why do so many marketers and advertising teams have trouble coming up with an idea that touches a consumer's heart?

They think too much. That's right. Just about every advertising agency that we have come across has developed its own process for being "insightful." Time and again we hear about a set of finely honed steps—usually involving a so-called proprietary methodology for mining consumers' innermost thoughts—designed to unearth the inner truths about consumers. But these formal processes usually miss, sometimes widely, because formulas, by definition, apply a similar set of rules to every product or circumstance, thereby ignoring the very tool that leads to great insights: intuition.

A host of recent research indicates that our intuition is much savvier and more reliable than most corporations would ever admit. Today, institutes from Harvard University to the U.S. Marine Corps support research on the power of our subconscious mind. "Many emotions are products of evolutionary wisdom, which probably has more intelligence than all human minds together," says New York University neural scientist Joseph LeDoux in his book *The Emotional Brain: The Mysterious Underpinnings of Emotional Life*. Timothy D. Wilson, professor of psychology at the University of Virginia, ran a study that revealed that people who chose a poster for their living room wall on gut instinct were much happier with their choice than people who deliberated over the decision. Reporting on this finding and others, Sharon Begley in the *Wall Street Journal* noted that "there is a growing consensus that the unconscious is a pretty smart cookie, with cognitive capacities that rival and sometimes surpass that of conscious thought." Picasso claimed that his genius resided in his intuitive self when he said, "Painting is stronger than I am. It makes me do what it wants."

Instincts are smart, argues researcher Gary Klein in his recently published *Intuition at Work: Why Developing Your Gut Instincts Will Make You Better at What You Do,* because they are "not accidental. They reflect your experience." To Klein, our intuition is based on pattern recognition and subtle clues from experience that we may be unable to articulate, but that inform our gut instincts. According to Dr. Steve Hymowitz, a New York psychotherapist specializing in hypnosis, these hundreds and thousands of life experiences accumulate in our unconscious, creating an intelligence that has the capacity to surpass conscious thought. He compares the conscious and subconscious mind to a computer. "The conscious mind—like a computer screen—can handle five to nine chunks of information at any given point. The unconscious can hold limitless information, like the hard drive of a computer. And literally everything that is stored can be accessed by hitting the right button."

Many legendary marketing campaigns came about because the

final decision maker decided to trust his intuition. "If a strategy comes from the mind," says Maurice Lévy, chairman and CEO of Publicis Groupe, our parent company, "then ideas come from the guts." When MasterCard's "Priceless" campaign was first launched, its ads scored below average on *USA Today*'s closely watched Ad Track consumer rating index. MasterCard's marketing chief Larry Flanagan, ignoring the research, persisted with the campaign. He instinctively knew that the commercials got to the heart of those values that money can't buy—values that he was convinced consumers felt were important. And his intuition was right. Eventually, the campaign gained traction, and the spots went on to become a huge hit, helping to narrow the gap between MasterCard and market leader Visa.

The change Volvo made in its advertising approach is another example of the wisdom of intuition. In the early 1980s, Bob Schmetterer, now CEO of global advertising agency Euro RSCG Worldwide, was the partner in charge of Volvo at Scali, McCabe, Sloves. At the time, says Schmetterer, Volvo was positioned as "a high-quality, well-built, last-forever kind of car." But Schmetterer, after doing some exploratory research, had a gut instinct that safety might be a better way for Volvo to appeal to its potential buyers. "We discovered a hidden reality. Most Volvos at that time were being bought by men, but they were being *driven* by women. We figured that women are very interested in safety, particularly if they have young children on board."

The conventional wisdom at the time, however, was that people don't buy cars based on safety. Instead, they choose cars based on sex appeal, power, or reliability. "Ford had tried back in the 1960s to sell cars on safety, by focusing on seatbelts, and it was a disaster," remembers Schmetterer. "The conventional wisdom was that people bought cars because they look great, they fit their personality, or they can afford them." Consequently, the people at Volvo were initially cool to Schmetterer's idea about safety.

"But I pushed very hard," Schmetterer recalls. "I said, 'Listen.

You've already developed a position based on how well built the car is. People already believe that. But safety is bigger. It's the ultimate end benefit of a well-built car.'"

Volvo began to buy into that strategy and by the early 1990s Schmetterer and his partners at Messner, Vetere, Berger, McNamee, Schmetterer, Euro RSCG presented a series of commercials that were testimonials by people who revealed that their life had been saved by their Volvo. The original tagline was "Drive safely"— often the last words we say when a friend or relative leaves the house to drive home.

Volvo finally agreed to run the campaign, and Donald Sutherland signed on to become the voice behind the ads. They succeeded beyond the company's wildest dreams. Volvo was soon the car of choice in suburban driveways. "The result was great for Volvo in terms of sales, but more important," says Schmetterer, "they now own the position of arguably the safest car in the world."

In an era when cold, hard facts rule the day, senior management and marketers are reluctant to just trust their instincts. Having "good instincts" usually means introducing messy emotions, which is anathema to today's rational businessperson. "When I come into a business situation," says Dr. Ona Robinson, "I see how terrified most employees are of their feelings. I change my whole dialogue when I work with a company. People feel vulnerable if they show their feelings in a business situation."

At KTG, intuition has been our secret weapon. We recognize from many years of experience that our best ideas stem from an original creative impulse. Of course, we would never argue that facts, research, and left-brain thinking aren't crucial to the development of a Big Bang. They are. The difference is that *we put intuition first*. During the creative process, we encourage employees of KTG to listen to their inner voices to come up with ideas. Only then do we put our rational mind to work, to vet the idea and evaluate its merits. As nineteenth-century mathematician Henri Poincaré put it, "It is by logic that we prove. But it is by intuition that we discover."

How do we harness the power of intuition to come up with Big Bang marketing ideas? Here are some of the techniques we use:

Stop Ignoring Your Feminine Side

Perhaps the reason we at KTG are so successful at tapping into the consumer psyche is that we're a firm run by women. There's enough estrogen around our offices to make Arnold Schwarzenegger ovulate. Perhaps because of that, we aren't afraid to make big decisions by following our gut. Feminine instinct, we believe, is no myth. "Women's intuition has been scientifically tested and measured since the 1980s and, for the most part, comes down to a woman's superiority in all the perceptive senses," claim Barbara and Allan Pease in *Why Men Don't Listen and Woman Can't Read Maps.* David G. Myers, in *Intuition: Its Powers and Perils,* seems to agree, stating that there is a "gender intuition gap," that "women generally surpass men at decoding emotional messages." He cites research that says that although boys average 45 points higher on the SAT math tests, "girls surpass boys in reading facial expressions."

Bring Your Blankie

Let people rely on whatever idiosyncratic peccadilloes help them think. I can only write emotional scripts while listening to Irish folk tunes played on a pan flute; a colleague must have plush toys on hand to squish while he's working. No matter how unprofessional it seems, if you allow people to surround themselves with comforting props, their creative juices will flow like water.

Women may have developed better intuitive powers as a defense mechanism, honed over centuries as the weaker sex: If I can't beat you up, I somehow have to figure you out to get what I want. Or maybe it stems from the maternal instinct, the ability to quickly figure out what babies want so they will survive (or at least stop crying at 2 A.M!). "As childbearers and nest defenders," say the Peases, women "needed the ability to sense subtle mood and attitude changes in others. What is commonly called 'women's intuition' is mostly a woman's acute ability to notice small details and changes in the appearance or behavior of others." This search for a competitive advantage is hardly unique to Homo sapiens. Researchers studying elephants in Africa made a startling discovery while observing boy and girl twin elephants. When going to nurse, the male would simply butt the female out of the way. As a result, the female rapidly learned to nurse when the male was sleeping, playing, or otherwise occupied. In other words, to survive she had to be clever.

Stop Thinking About the Business

The classical model of decision making, taught in business schools around the country, is based on analysis and logic; managers evaluate options based on a set of criteria about the issue at hand. It all sounds very scientific, says intuition researcher Gary Klein, and "comforting. Who would not want to be thorough, systematic, rational and scientific?" he writes.

"The only problem is that the whole thing is a myth. . . . It doesn't do so well in the real world, where decisions are more challenging, situations are more confusing and complex, information is scarce or inconclusive, time is short and stakes are high. And in that environment, the classical, analytical model of decision making falls flat."

Randi Dorman, group director at Interbrand, a New York City–based brand-identity consulting firm, agrees. Working with

Forget About the Forest

A new project can seem overwhelming at times. Facts, figures, and intellectual chatter can freeze you in your tracks. Taking a page from Eastern meditation, we prefer to start small. We often start with just the first small step, moving from one detail to the next. In the process of moving forward, we usually stumble upon the solution to the big picture.

brands such as Crest, which relies on packaging to grab the consumer's attention in the supermarket aisle, she encourages her clients to think about "shelf interest" rather than "shelf impact." While package designers traditionally rely on loud graphics and the age-old "new and improved!" approach, Dorman insists that's not enough. "If you go to the supermarket, there are aisles and aisles of products, and there is so much to look at. It's created kind of a loud wallpaper that has led to a grab-and-go mentality. They know the products they like so they grab and go as quickly as possible.

"But it's not enough to be loud and impactful at the shelf," Dorman continues. "You have to do something more intriguing. You have to speak to something that's going on in the consumer's life, that speaks to what the consumer is looking for and how she might be changing. And you have to make it easy for her to shop."

Dorman cites Campbell's soup as an example of a manufacturer that hasn't focused enough on consumer needs, and as a result, they've missed the mark both emotionally and with regards to shopability. "If you go to the soup aisle, you see condensed soup, chunky soup, and ready-to-serve soup, and it's all so confusing.

You can tell that they've been doing everything based on what different things they can make versus making it easy for the consumer to find what they want."

I, unfortunately, have an example of how this kind of rational thinking can lead you astray.

Bad Medicine

In early 2000, we were vying with another agency to win the Bristol-Myers Squibb corporate account. Bristol-Myers Squibb is one of the leading manufacturers of cancer drugs, among other things, and we heard plenty from CEO Peter Dolan about how Tour de France champion Lance Armstrong had beaten a deadly cancer by taking drugs created in the company's labs.

One day while we were brainstorming ideas for the campaign, Laurie Garnier, our global creative director for Clairol, came into my office and said, "Forgive me. I know I'm not directly working on this, but I gotta tell you that this Lance Armstrong guy is something. He's alive because of those drugs. You really should do a spot with him." She told me the story of Armstrong and how his wife recently gave birth to his son.

I got my legendary chills, my unconscious reaction to a Big Bang idea. But then I started to think. I said, "Yeah, it is an incredible story. But I don't know, it's so obvious. Everyone's going to use him."

She went away, undaunted, and came back with a script. She said to me, "Linda, this guy had this unbelievably deadly cancer. He shouldn't even be alive. And now he's got this baby . . ."

I sat down and considered whether we should use Armstrong as a spokesperson. Eventually, I came up with a rational, sensible list of reasons why Armstrong wouldn't work. One, he'd been used in other ad campaigns, so he might not be clearly identified with Bristol-Myers Squibb. Testimonials have been done a lot—the company is going to want something more unexpected. Besides, I thought, what if Armstrong loses the next Tour de France? And anyway, the focus is too narrow. Bristol-Myers Squibb isn't just a cancer-drug company, they make baby formula and Exedrin and a ton of other miracle drugs. So instead we came up with a much more generic corporate campaign.

To my embarrassment, we lost the account to the other agency. And guess what their campaign featured? Lance Armstrong, who was alive because of the drugs from Bristol-Myers Squibb, bouncing his beautiful baby son. The spot brought tears to everybody's eyes—especially mine, as I mourned the lost account.

Thinking over my mistake, I felt like an idiot. I knew in my gut that everybody loves a story with a happy ending, even if they've heard it again and again. But instead of trusting my instincts, I had focused on all the rational reasons why we should do something else. And it was a big mistake.

Stop Listening

Sometimes we're so focused on what someone says that we forget to read the other person's nuances and gestures. As Barbara and Allan Pease put it in their book *Why Men Don't Listen and Women Can't Read Maps,* "in face-to-face communications, nonverbal signals account for 60 to 80 percent of the impact of the message, while vocal sounds make up 20 to 30 percent. The other 7 to 10 percent is words." If an employer asks a staff member if she's happy that day, and she replies "Yes," it's that much easier to ignore the body signals that shout out how miserable she's feeling. Language can conceal and obfuscate as well as clarify and elaborate. Frequently, in business, language asks us to take the answers we hear at face value, when often the real communication isn't one that has been put into words at all.

By paying attention to nonverbal cues, you can learn volumes about what a client, a CEO, or division leader is really saying. We all have the capacity and skill to do this; it's been bred into our bones since the first caveman stopped his enemy in his tracks with

> ### Emotion Aerobics
>
> If you want people to tap into the consumer's unconscious, you need to help your staff tap into their feelings. We do this several ways: One, I start most creative meetings with a joke. Humor takes pressure off of people and draws people together. Laughing disarms and relaxes us. It also stimulates the limbic system, the part of the brain that is most involved in emotions. At other meetings, I'll begin by relating a deeply emotional event—often something I've read in the morning paper. The empathy elicited from the group can work in the same way, making them more primed for the work we're doing.

a mere grimace. A recent study published in the *Proceedings of the National Academy of Sciences,* for example, suggests that we all have the innate ability to distinguish cheats. Psychologist Jennifer Voigt Kaplan concurs with its findings: "Prehistoric humans had a better chance of survival if they could identify cheats so that they were not robbed out of food, mates, supplies, and so forth. The humans who survived possessed this quality and handed it down to their kids. So from the angle of using instincts to size people up," she concludes, "you can make a case for why we should listen to our instincts."

Brand expert Randi Dorman remembers working on the design for Red Zone antiperspirant, a high-performance product by Old Spice. "Instead of listening to all the research stuff about the deodorant business, we decided to see who is able to get through to men," she recalls, "because men aren't as sophisticated at the drugstore or supermarket as women." They decided to look at business that did speak successfully to men. "We looked at everything from car batteries to fishing line to lights to socks. We looked at the colors and textures that they like, from sports cars to diamond-plated steel to Mack trucks, and we used that for inspiration." The resulting logo is macho brushed silver with rivets in it, with a background that echoes the design at the end of a drill bit. "These are textures that speak to guys, and made Red Zone relevant to its target audience."

When you are meeting with a client, whether the client is in-house or from another company, it's crucial that you be aware of what *isn't* said. Of course you must pay attention and listen to the information, but you must also heed your inner voice. That is where you may find the inside story that needs to be told.

Truth on Tap

When I was at Wells, Rich, Greene, we were invited to pitch Heineken to win its advertising business. During our briefing meeting, when the Heineken management was telling us about the company, we were given loads of promotional materials and statistics, all of which we hoped would be helpful in developing a campaign. As the presentation got under way, Michael Foley, the president of Heineken at the time, started walking around the room, spouting off facts about the hops and the barley and the special Heineken yeast that had been around for a hundred years.

Up to then, I had never had a beer in my life, so I started to tune Foley's speech out. Instead I just watched him circle the room. He was proudly holding a bottle of beer high in the air, like the Statue of Liberty, never once putting the bottle down. Flush with emotion, he quoted the company's flamboyant CEO, Freddie Heineken, who said, "I don't sell beer, I sell warmth." I knew right then that the beer was the least of what Heineken, and Michael Foley, were about, whatever they might say.

I went back to my office and reported to my staff: "This guy doesn't think he has a beer, he thinks he has a piece of pop culture. He thinks he's got a Kodak. That's the point we have to get across in our advertising." I told them to throw out everything that they were working on for the account. "I don't want anything that feels like beer. None of that typical jock stuff with girls and sports. No talk of imported hops or filtered mountain spring water." My staff protested, and reminded me that they had great funny ads. "Every other agency will have great funny ads," I retorted.

Instead, Douglas Atkin, our strategic planner at the time, went into action. He spent the next two weeks visiting bars to find out exactly how people felt about their beer, and how it was intertwined with their lives. "We even used an anthropologist to conduct focus groups of people who drank beer," remembers Atkin.

He discovered that "when people drink, they go through a rite of passage. They enter this rite of passage with their social personas on, whatever they'd adopted to get on in the world. As you drink your inhibitions go down and you start behaving—or it feels this way to the person drinking—on a more authentic level." Drinking beer, in the minds of its fans, strips away anxieties and pretenses and allows you to become your core self: honest, uncensored, unpretentious. It enables you to say and do things with an honesty you might never be able to muster otherwise.

Not only that, but nearly everybody associated the Heineken brand with truth and authenticity, not least because its recipe has been unchanged for over one hundred years. "Most American beer is seen as inauthentic because they throw all sorts of things in them," Atkin says. "But European beer is authentic because it just has four ingredients: water, hops, yeast, and malted barley. Heineken is one of those, and it comes from northern Europe, the center of beer-making in Europe. It has provenance, the right location, and history, all of which makes it authentic. It tastes real."

We realized then that the advertising had to say that Heineken is a cultural icon, a symbol of truth. It was an authentic activity done with an authentic brand. This beer is the real thing. And so the "True Conversations," campaign was created—a series of ads based on real conversations from bars. The ads featured no cleavage, no sports, and no people (so that guys twenty-one *and* forty-one would identify with the spot). There wasn't even a mention of the beer. The campaign consisted of shots of bars, closeups of beer being poured, the Heineken logo, accompanied by charming exchanges like this:

> *Man's voice:* "You don't know who wrote *Moby Dick?*"
>
> *Woman's voice:* "No."
>
> *Man:* "You don't know who wrote *Moby Dick.*"
>
> *Woman:* "Nnnoo."
>
> *Man:* "The one with the whale."
>
> *Woman:* "I saw the movie."
>
> *Man:* "But you never read the book."
>
> *Woman:* "So what?"
>
> *Man:* "So what? It's *Moby Dick.*"
>
> *Woman:* "Look. I don't know who the [beep] wrote *Moby* [beep]-ing *Dick.* OK?
>
> *Man:* [Long pause]. OK.
>
> *Type superimposed on the ad:* Their words. Their beer. It's all true.
>
> *Tagline (as the Heineken logo flashes on the screen):* True to the original recipe since 1886.
>
> *Final tagline:* Herman Melville.

The ad won us the account. It was unlike anything that Heineken, or any other beer company for that matter, had ever done. It was a hugely risky move, because we were only allowed to show one idea to the client. If we failed, we failed. Moroever, it didn't address a single goal laid out by the company at our briefing meeting, yet it hit upon the one authentic thing about Heineken behind the president's spiel. It spoke directly to his belief that their product did more than quench thirst or take the edge off a tough day. It was an icon of purity and honesty in a dishonest, impure world.

And it all came about because we had a hunch that overrode the avalanche of marketing materials given to us by the client. Many agencies, in fact, would never have let someone with no experience drinking or marketing beer into the room with Foley. But the fact that I didn't know a whole a lot about the business enabled me to move away from the traditional and expected. I had no emotional baggage. Naturally we tested the concept with beer aficionados after the fact, but the original concept stemmed from a gut response to Foley's behavioral clues.

Stop Trying to Be Smart

Plenty of creative advertising and marketing folks like to display their intelligence in their work. Look how clever I am, their work seems to shout out. This is rarely a smart move. Maurice Lévy remembers a campaign from the early 1980s, when a drink called Green Sands was debuted in France. "We did one of those cutting-edge commercials, directed by Tony Scott, the very latest in trendiness at the time. And the success lasted what a fashion season lasts: one summer."

We actively shy away from trendiness. The work isn't about us, it's about embracing the consumer. In fact, we get a fair amount of grief for being an agency that relies on broad humor and sentimentality. But as Stuart Elliott, advertising columnist for the *New York Times* pointed out about me in a recent column, I "unapologetically embrace [my] image as a throwback to when ads tugged at heartstrings and poked at funny bones rather than taking postmodern, hipper-than-thou postures."

Doria Steedman, an executive vice president with Partnership for a Drug-Free America, argues that by relying on straightforward yet compelling stories, her organization has greatly increased its visibility. In 1995 the partnership came out with an ad that tried to explain a simple fact about sniffing inhalants—albeit in a graphic way. A little girl is sitting in a sweet little-girl bedroom and all of a sudden water starts to pour into the room. As the room fills up with water, she floats to the window and struggles to get out, but drowns. The voiceover talks about the inhalants, and says, "So when you think you're sniffing, your brain thinks it's drowning. And your brain is pretty much right." It wasn't a commercial that tried to flaunt gimmicks or cleverness; rather, it just focused on getting across the simple idea that this drug hurts your body.

Play Dumb

Creativity depends on collaboration, which won't happen if you're intent on being the smartest person in the room. Encourage people to let down their intellectual pretenses and hear what the other guy is saying. Only then can they be receptive to ideas. Act dumb, if you must. When Procter & Gamble CEO A. G. Lafley is presented with an overly complicated press release or report, he says, "Give me the *Sesame Street* version." Each time you say, "I don't understand," you force people to distill their idea down to a simple and clear concept. If your creative solution can't be communicated to a four-year-old, chances are the Secaucus bowling league won't get it either. Take your next idea home to your kids, and if they don't get it in one simple sentence, go back to the drawing board.

While it is difficult to track the effectiveness of such ads, Steedman points to research that indicates that it was at least partly responsible for a downturn in use.

Years ago, when I was working on Kodak at J. Walter Thompson, my desire to zero in on age-old instincts helped lead me to one of my first Big Bangs.

A number of us were asked to develop a campaign for the Kodak disc camera, a new camera that eliminated the need for cartridge film. The disc camera had taken years for the Eastman Kodak chemical engineers to develop. Instead of having to feed the film to the camera and advance it every time you took a picture, you just plopped a wafer-thin disc in, took pictures, and popped it out when it was done. It was kind of like a toaster oven for negatives.

But much of the advertising the agency proposed using was technical and graphic, full of flashing laser lights, a somber homage to all those engineers hunched over processing baths. This advertising made the camera seem as formidable as IBM's Deep Blue super computer at a chess match.

My colleagues spent a lot of time talking to the Kodak people, and they were up to their eyeballs in facts and figures about the science that went into the camera. I, fortunately, had not delved into all the research. The minute I saw the Kodak disc camera, my gut reaction was that this was the perfect PhD camera (Push Here, Dummy); it should be marketed to moms, kids, grandparents, just about anybody who knew nothing about taking pictures. The disc camera, with all its complexity, was an incredibly simple camera to use.

So I decided to write a simple jingle that highlighted the fact that the camera was easy to operate. The song was entitled "I'm Gonna Getcha with the Kodak Disc," and featured kids and parents snapping each other with a mere flick of the wrist. Kodak loved it, and decided to go with it. Although some of the Kodak marketing folks were absolutely incensed over this nonsensical little ditty—how dare we use it to peddle their scientific masterpiece—the advertising certainly helped develop a pretty picture for the camera's sales results.

Stop Acting Your Age

A radio talk show host once commented that inside every middle-aged person sipping coffee or tea, there's an eight-year-old child slurping ice cream. Our inner child is where many of our most imaginative and uncensored selves lie. As such, it is an embryonic breeding ground for Big Bang ideas. It's the romper room where our minds roam unfettered and free, where feelings rule the landscape. In *Riding the Tiger: Doing Business in a Transforming World* Harrison Owen says, "In play, we are enabled to do in pretend time (a time/space continuum of our own making) what is either impossible, unthinkable, or dangerous to do in real time. Then, it sometimes occurs that the line between 'pretend' and 'real' is removed, and somehow the impossible, unthinkable, and dangerous become common practice. This is called innovation and creativity."

Unfortunately, the pretensions of adult habits, conventions, and behavior tend to stifle creativity. Roger von Oech, who runs workshops on creativity and is the author of the million-copy bestseller *A Whack on the Side of the Head,* claims that we are trained to toe the line the minute we enter school, where the system insists there's just one right answer, when often there are many. "If you think there is only one right answer, then you'll stop looking as soon as you find one."

But tuning in to your playful side can yield great results. Let me give you an example. When *Vanity Fair* magazine was brought back to life in 1983, it was relaunched as a high-minded literary magazine, filled with lengthy, highbrow articles and serious literature. It was also anything but popular. Then owner Condé Nast decided to hire British editor Tina Brown, who changed the approach of the magazine by appealing to the teenager in all of us. She filled it with tabloid crime tales, starlets du jour, and gossipy stories about the "popular" kids. In doing so, she turned the magazine into one of the industry's biggest success stories.

Big Bangs like this happen more easily when you nurture your childlike side. Roy J. Bostock, retired chairman of the McManus Group and now chairman of Partnership for a Drug-Free America, was in charge of the agency that created the original Budweiser frog commercials. Bostock remembers chatting with the two guys who came up with the idea and asking them what their inspiration was. "They told me that they knew they needed to come up with an idea that would really resonate with twenty-one to twenty-eight-year-old guys," Bostock recalls. "For some reason, they started talking about their youth and the things that they liked when they were kids." Soon they were both reliving the days when they would spend hours catching and playing with frogs. "Suddenly they realized that they had to use a frog in the Bud ads." This connection to childhood resulted in one of the best pieces of ad-

Sweet Spots

People at KTG have noticed that I always seem to laugh at art director Whitney Pillsbury's ideas. One day, he confessed his secret to me: He plops a bowl of M&Ms in front of me before he reads me his scripts. He figured out that when I'm eating chocolates, I'm happier and predisposed to like his work. (He also happens to be one of the funniest humans alive.) It turns out that it's not just me: Chocolate has over 300 chemicals in it, including caffeine, theobromine, and phenylethylamine—all substances that stimulate the neurotransmitters in our brains that control our ability to concentrate. If you want to help win over a client or boss on your Big Bang campaign, give someone on staff the job of making sure every meeting starts with some sweet incentives.

vertising ever to resonate with young men, one of the most coveted demographic targets for television ads.

Adults require this loosening up to unleash the creative ideas that lurk in our imaginations. I discovered this in 1981, when I was a junior copywriter at J. Walter Thompson, with a cubicle office about the size of a dollar bill, and a salary to match. I was chomping at the bit to work on the Toys "R" Us pitch that our agency was invited to participate in. Perhaps because I had not let go of the child within me, I created one of the Biggest Bangs of my career.

I Won't Grow Up

At the time, Toys "R" Us was looking for a new agency. Toys "R" Us stores, like those of its competitors Child World (doomed eventually to extinction in the wake of Charles Lazarus's brilliant business acumen) and K-B Toys, were really just big warehouses for toys. It became painfully obvious to us that a Barbie was a Barbie was a Barbie, no matter where you bought it. We knew we had to create an image for the store that did everything but actually show the store, which was vast, intimidating, and had the warmth of Howe Caverns. Somehow we had to let consumers feel that when you bought your toy at Toys "R" Us, you were bringing something much more valuable home.

Our team went out and bought a bunch of toys for, ah, research purposes, brought them back to our offices, and starting looking them over. Soon we were playing with them, and unable to put them down. And that's when the Big Bang idea hit us like a hockey puck in the head: Toys make you feel like a kid again. And that feels good. So good, we thought, that why would anyone want to grow up?

James Patterson, the executive creative director, and Deyna Vesey, my art director, came up with the line "I Don't Wanna Grow Up, I'm a Toys 'R' Us Kid." But we needed something besides a theme line to truly make the strategy sing. What it needed, I realized, was a song.

This was right up my Tin Pan Alley. I have a master's degree in musicology (which, for those of you unfamiliar with the titillating excitement of academia, is the history of music from the pan flute on), and had composed several children's songs as well as some off-off-(boy-were-they-off)-Broadway shows. Nonetheless, the odds of authoring the jingle that would win the account and eventually air on national television were slimmer than my paycheck. In fact, we went to a number of music houses, and each eagerly submitted songs in the hopes of winning the hefty residual payments that come with a widely advertised campaign. Even Tony-award-winning composer Charles Strouse (*Annie* and *Bye Bye Birdie*) did a tune on spec for us. Of course, the obvious answer was the hit song "I Won't Grow Up" from the musical *Peter Pan* (for which the copyright holders wanted $100,000).

But none of the fifteen or so demos we received got our toes tapping. So I just started fooling around on my keyboard one day, and came up with a childlike little ditty that I thought might appeal to kids. My boss didn't really like it, but he agreed to air it for the client. As it turned out, the Toys "R" Us folks loved it (not least because it didn't cost them anything to own). Moreover, when the song was tested on little kids, it got a resounding thumbs-up (from those who could get their thumbs out of their mouths, that is).

One week after the song officially aired on national television, my boss confessed that he had made a mistake about the song.

"What made you change your mind?" I asked.

"Well," he said, "I was getting my coffee at Logan airport yesterday, and the waiter was humming your tune."

Two weeks later I heard a kid singing it on the street. His mother yelled at him that if he didn't stop singing that silly song, they were going to miss the bus! I wanted to kiss him!

Twenty-two years later, "I Don't Wanna Grow Up, I'm a Toys 'R' Us Kid" continues to be the store's theme song in their television and radio ads. Virtually every kid across the country (and their parents as well) can sing the jingle. If you visit the flagship store in Manhattan's Times Square, you'll hear over a dozen differ-

"I'M A TOYS 'R' US KID" IS ONE OF THE LONGEST RUNNING JINGLES IN ADVERTISING.

ent arrangements broadcast in different departments. The tune has become one of the longest airing jingles in advertising history.

Why did it work? Well, it's a good jingle, I think. But it's also about a state of mind, about reminding you what it's like to be a kid again. By bringing out the child in all of us during those creative meetings, we unleashed an idea that tapped into the six-year-old who lives on in all of us.

Stop Being Cool

Being hip in marketing is often the kiss of death. Trends come and go. That means they can become outdated in a nanosecond. And being cool is frankly alienating: Everyone who feels they aren't in the know will turn their back on your message. As a result, a trendy ad limits the number of people it will connect with.

Let me give you a case in point. Several years ago Norwegian Cruise Line ran a campaign called "It's Different Out Here." The ads were very simple and ethereal, with avant-garde black-and-white close-ups of lush island scenery, undulating water, and glamorous couples lounging about. Everyone in advertising raved about the ads, and they won many accolades. The problem? They didn't sell cruises. Consumers could make neither heads nor tails of them. "Every frame of those ads was frameable," then-marketing VP Nina Cohen said, "but we're not in the framing business." She hired a new agency and soon the company went back to more traditional ads that talked about big cabins, out-of-the-way locales, good food—things that cruise vacationers could relate to.

When Continental Airlines relaunched its business in the mid-1990s, the company didn't run glitzy advertising. Most of the airline companies at the time were still running ads with planes flying through clouds, recalls Bonnie Reitz, former senior vice president of marketing, sales, and distribution at Continental. "Some of the ads were even more abstract, with shots of balloons flying through the air with messages on them," she says. Continental, however, decided "to be very simple and truthful and talk to customers about what is important to them," says Reitz. They understood that frequent fliers want consistency, comfort, and convenience. That's it—over and out. No surprises. Not even bargain basement value. With their "Work Hard, Fly Right" campaign, they sent the message that they serve the real-life needs of their bread-and-butter customers, the business traveler. As a result, they have become one of the biggest turnaround stories of our time. They are now the number-one airline out of New York and regularly beat every one of their competitors on customer satisfaction surveys.

Some marketing executives are so focused on being arch that they ignore the reason for the ad in the first place: to enhance the brand. "Some people who create TV advertising feel like the brand name gets in the way of what they're trying to do," says Gerry Lukeman, chairman emeritus of Ipsos-ASI, a Connecticut-based ad-

THESE CLEVER DESTINATION ADS, LIKE THIS ONE FOR THE FLIGHT FROM NEW YORK TO TEL AVIV, HELPED GIVE CONTINENTAL ITS SMART, NO-NONSENSE IMAGE.

vertising research firm, "so they stick it on, rather reluctantly, just at the end of the commercial. They're doing the ad less for the brand and more for the art. When you look at a lot of this stuff, it seems to me quite a few people on the creative side are in the business of creating 30-second foreign films. Anything that gets in the way of that is considered an obstacle."

Instead of concentrating on being cutting edge, we feel it's much more important to stick to the basics that never go out of style. Get in tune with people's souls. In fact, we think you have to make a conscious effort to try *not* to be hip, or get distracted by fads. As Maurice Lévy, CEO of Publicis Groupe, said in a recent *New York Times* interview, "There are people who do advertising for what I call the advertising village and people who are doing advertising for the consumer." We've been successful because we focus exclusively on creating marketing for the *consumer*. That is why we exist—to help companies sell themselves, and sell their products.

The key is to find the truth you are trying to convey to your audience—and finding a way to express that truth through emotion.

This is a philosophy I relied on when I was asked to help out with the advertising for Bill Clinton's first presidential campaign in 1992. This was in the wake of the Gennifer Flowers story, and Mandy Grunwald, one of Clinton's political strategists, realized Clinton needed some good old-fashioned emotional appeal.

Friend of Bill

By September 1992, there were enough seedy stories swirling about Bill Clinton that Grunwald wanted to remind the voters of Clinton's Horatio Alger struggle from poor boy in Hope, Arkansas, to presidential candidate.

I was asked to create a sixty-second biographical spot that would run a few weeks before the election. Up until then, the usual bio fare in political ads was cluttered with flashy fanfare, empty platitudes, and endless lists of bills the candidate backed or supported. But for an already suspicious public, we needed a film that would connect people emotionally to Clinton, a message that convinced voters he would "Put People First." The tabloids' innuendos made Clinton look unelectable; but after meeting him, my gut told me something quite different. I became convinced that Clinton was a man who cared about the ordinary guy, and passionately believed in the causes he espoused. My challenge was to find a way to let Americans see that side as well.

I filled the spot with scrapbook memories, including footage of Bill at seventeen shaking President Kennedy's hand, faded shots of his grandparents' store in Hope, Arkansas, innocent black-and-white photos of his humble small-town beginnings. And then I edited it in slooooow mooooootion, because nothing moves people like people moving slowly. Watch an old video of your grandfather prancing around on your first birthday and he looks like a character actor in *One Flew Over the Cuckoo's Nest*. But play the film back in slo-mo and suddenly he's a cinematic lion in winter, and you find your eyes welling up with tears. It's a hackneyed gimmick, but it works.

The spot I created accomplished two things: It helped us all believe once again in the American dream, that anything is possible. After all, look where this guy had come from, the spot seemed to say, and look where he's going! The spot also made Clinton more human, which made his rumored transgressions more forgivable. It was the perfect antidote to all the cynicism in the press at the time.

After I completed the spot and sent it over, one of the producers called me. "I hope you're sitting down," he said. He went on to tell me that the governor had been playing the videotape over and over again. He was actually crying. He had never seen his life portrayed in such an emotional way before. Most of the ads up to that point had been a somewhat clinical list of his accomplishments. As Mandy Grunwald later told *USA Today*, this ad was different. "We viewed the ad for the first time and realized it was perfect—touching, moving. It's rare when that happens."

THIS PROPHETIC FOOTAGE, PART OF A COMMERCIAL FOR CLINTON'S 1992
CAMPAIGN, WENT STRAIGHT FOR THE CONSUMER'S GUT.

Stop Denying Your Feelings

Emotion is universal. Instead of trying to think about what's funny
to soccer moms in Peoria, think about what's funny to *you*. Instead
of guessing what will get a blue-collar father of two choked up,
think about what puts a lump in *your* throat. You may think you are
of a higher order than Anna Nicole Smith, but here's the unvar-
nished truth: We all share 99.9 percent of the same genes. We are
all startlingly alike. So get over it.

The fact is that old-fashioned emotions spring from basic
truths. They don't change with the seasons. Say hello to someone
in Botswana and you'll be met with a blank stare. But share pictures of your children, and you'll make a friend for life. So chances
are good that if an idea makes you laugh, it'll make others laugh. If
it makes me cry, it'll make you cry too.

Big Bangs happen when you connect with a primary emotion. Why is the Volkswagon Beetle such a hit? Margaret Mark and Carol S. Pearson, authors of *The Hero and the Outlaw: Building Extraordinary Brands Through the Power of Archetypes,* argue that it appeals to one of our most universal feelings: "Looking at the design through the archetypal lens, we see that the 'face' of the new Beetle is virtually identical to the face of an infant—with big eyes and a high, smooth forehead. Research has shown that throughout both the animal and the human kingdom, those same baby-faced characteristics, the characteristics of the Innocent, signal that there is no threat and that the creature is in need of care. . . . They are faces that win hearts the world over."

Dye Laughing

I have always counted on basic emotions to connect with my audience. In the early 1990s, when I was at J. Walter Thompson, we landed the Clairol account. I was asked to come up with some commercials for Nice 'n Easy, billed as an entry-level hair color for people who were a bit hesitant to color their hair.

Nice 'n Easy was doing terribly at the time, not least because of the current campaign, which was very apologetic. Basically the ads said, Don't worry, people won't notice, not much will change. I knew that this was the wrong approach. "Look," I said to the folks at Clairol, "You're making this so damn serious! It's not brain surgery, it's hair color, for God's sake. Women have children, we have breast cancer, we have deadbeat husbands! Coloring our hair is the least of our problems!"

I argued instead that we should make the whole hair-color concept a piece of funny business, and we proposed using Julia Louis-Dreyfus as the spokesperson. At the time, Louis-Dreyfus was in a funny but relatively unknown show called *Seinfeld.* "Her character, Elaine, is the girl next door, she's cute, a little sarcastic, attractive but not too pretty. She's someone women would like to talk to, not some ice-queen supermodel," I explained to the Clairol folks.

135

The executive I was working with responded, "Over my dead body will I have a comedienne who's a brunette, and not a model, pitching and selling our hair color." But I had that familiar feeling in my gut that this was a Big Bang. So I refused to let it go. I took the idea to other people at Clairol.

Finally I found Peter Spengler, a top executive at Bristol-Myers Squibb, who knew of *Seinfeld*; after much wheedling and begging, and the support of Steve Sadove, the former president of Clairol, they convinced the marketing director to take a risk. We didn't even bother doing a test, we just went ahead and shot the commercials. And they were very funny. In one of them Louis-Dreyfus blathers on about how lucky she is to have been born with such naturally beautiful hair, then whispers confidentially to the viewers, "It's Natural Deep Brown 121."

Within a week after the commercial aired, sales skyrocketed and Natural Deep Brown 121 couldn't be found on the shelves.

We followed up with an ad where Louis-Dreyfus is riding a city bus; she transforms a mousy brown-haired woman into a fabulous blond right there on the M2. At the end of the commercial, our new blond bombshell is sent off the bus by Louis-Dreyfus with the line, "You're gonna stop traffic," at which point the viewer hears a resounding crash. The commercials were instant hits, catapulting Nice 'n Easy sales to an all-time high and helping to regain its position as the category leader at the time.

This experience brought home how effective a tool humor is in connecting with people. It was the first campaign in the category of women's beauty that used humor, and it worked like gangbusters. Through humor, the commercial said to all the women out there, "You know what, it's OK to color your hair. It's OK if everyone knows, and it's OK if it's obvious. It's fun!"

The flip side of humor, poignance, is another effective way to create a Big Bang. In 1997 AT&T ran a series of ads for its wireless phones. Instead of talking about the technology involved, however, or trying to explain some complicated minutes-per-week formula, the ads focused on the simple bonds of family and friends. In one memorable spot geared to guilt-ridden working moms, and set to Cyndi Lauper's hit *Girls Just Want to Have Fun,* a harried career mom is trying to get everyone out the door on a busy weekday morning. She's explaining to her daughter that she can't stop to talk because she's got a meeting with an important client. Her daughter looks at her and says, "When can I be a client?" Mom suddenly halts what she's doing, looks at her kids, and announces that today is a vacation day. The family heads to the beach, with Mom's trusty cell phone in tow just in case business comes up. The ads were the first telecom spots to make it into the top twenty most popular ads of *USA Today*'s Ad Track consumer index.

Tugging at heartstrings—as clichéd as it may seem—was the simple formula that Eastman Kodak rode all the way to the bank in the seventies and eighties. Back then, when I was the creative director working on the Kodak account, I knew that every ad I made had to do one thing when I showed it to the clients: bring tears to their eyes. It was that simple. Kodak was already an icon, and its marketing people completely grasped the importance of connecting with people's emotions. After all, Kodak was America's storyteller, the preserver of our memories, the product that was able to make time stand still.

So our team created ads that captured poignant moments everyone could relate to: "Daddy's Little Girl," by creative partners Mimi Emilita and Michael Hart, showed a dad dancing at his daughter's wedding, while nostalgically remembering images of her childhood. I created a spot with my art director, Greg Weinschenker, called "America," a motorcycle journey by a Vietnam vet rediscovering his country. The folksy song I wrote to go with it went on to win a Clio that year for Best Original Music with Lyrics.

The commercials were incredibly powerful, so much so that they were often more talked about than the TV shows they sponsored. Soon people began to call the touching instants in their lives "Kodak moments." Believe it or not, up to that time we had never used that phrase in our advertising. But it has since become part of the American vernacular, creating word-of-mouth advertising for the brand every time it's uttered.

My Own Kodak Moment

As basic and simple as these emotions are, coming up with Kodak moments wasn't always easy. In 1985 we were under the gun and desperately needed a new spot. But nothing was working. At the same time, my father's sixty-fifth birthday was looming, and I was having trouble thinking of a worthy present. Another necktie or gift certificate at RadioShack hardly seemed fitting to celebrate such a milestone. As the Kodak meeting and Dad's birthday drew closer, the dual dilemmas suddenly converged in me to create a Big Bang.

I gathered up all the old footage of my dad and family, and edited it into a movie, for which I wrote a song, "Dear Old Dad." On my dad's birthday, I asked him to turn on Channel 5 to watch one of our favorite old movies, *The Man in the Gray Flannel Suit,* starring Gregory Peck. My real reason for wanting him to watch became apparent when, in the middle of the show, a Kodak commercial came on. It began with a handwritten note that read, "To Dad, on his 65th birthday. Love, Linda." A two-minute video tribute followed, ending with a shot of a Kodak roll of film and the tagline: "When was the last time you took a picture of your dad?" Yes, I made my dad cry. But even more important, the ad made dads cry all over the country.

For years, Kodak ran a Father's Day spot with the same theme. That one connection of a daughter to her father sparked the memories of millions who saw it. It didn't seem obvious at the time, but what could be simpler than drawing from your own experience, from your own emotions?

When looking for a Big Bang, it sometimes helps to reach inside yourself, to tap into those emotions that supercede the inadequacies of language and thought, touching that place where our emotional DNA remains identical.

IMAGINE MY FATHER'S REACTION WHEN HE SAW THIS KODAK TWO-MINUTE TRIBUTE ON TELEVISION.

We've talked about the tools we've discovered that help to create Big Bang ideas: counterintuitive common sense, compression, chaos, intuition, becoming fluent in the language of emotions. And we've discussed how we go about creating an environment that fosters Big Bang ideas. Once you've come up with an in-box full of ideas, however, you still need to figure out which idea is the one with explosive power, the one that will go bang.

CHAPTER
6

WHAT GOES

bang?

When the apple fell on Isaac Newton's head (the story goes) he made a brilliant connection and discovered gravity. But few of us will recognize Big Bangs so easily. So how can you be sure that when a Big Bang idea crosses your desk, you'll see it?

In our chaotically creative offices, ideas are practically bouncing off the walls. Most, of course, are turkeys. Some are good. A few ideas are great. But even the great ideas may not be right. Some are too complicated to appeal to a mass market. Others are too expected. Some neglect a crucial detail. Some, though they may be fabulously funny or touching, may simply be off the mark. One of those Big Bang ideas, however, has the potential to take a product through the roof. And it is our job to figure out which one.

Coming up with great ideas is one thing; choosing the one that will strike gold is another. Sure, you need experience and intuition to help zero in on the top ideas or themes. Yet you can hardly ask a client to plunk down several million dollars just because a marketing campaign gives you goose bumps. It is at this point that you need to get clinical and put your ideas to the test.

The problem is, which test? There is no acid test for a Big Bang idea, no scientific method to isolate the one idea with legs. Until that campaign or product is cast out into the universe, we never know for certain whether or not it is the one that will explode.

That doesn't stop most marketing professionals from taking their top contenders through the traditional consumer testing paces—such as focus groups and recall tests—and scouring the results for proof that the idea will work. But we believe that this kind of market research tells only half the story, at best.

For one thing, a herd mentality sets in with vehicles such as focus groups. Who's going to admit that they like the tacky, sappy, wacky, or just plain weird in front of a bunch of other people? But this says little on how each of them would behave when alone in a store aisle. Rob Matteucci, who runs the hair-color business for Procter & Gamble, points out, for example, that very few men will admit to caring about their looks. "They feel that looks are as important as women do, but won't admit it. But I've seen it. They go through these routines with hairspray and the curling iron in the closet. Men are as obsessed about hair as most women. But you're not going to find this in research such as focus groups, because men won't admit it. In cases like this, research can actually be misleading. In order to get to guys in beauty care, we need to get to what's in their hearts, not listen to what they say with their mouths." While we believe that research tools such as focus groups have their place, we agree that their usefulness is limited.

Instead we rely heavily on ethnographic research, which marketers have borrowed from the social science of cultural anthropology. Often, the best way to learn from consumers is by watching them. You learn a lot about people's true feelings by observing the minutiae of how they interact with products and brands. Yes, this kind of observation is subjective, qualitative research. But we believe that we can learn more by closely observing how fifteen people use their watch than by throwing five watches in front of fifty or a hundred people and asking them which one they like.

We go into homes, out into the streets, into retail stores and businesses to analyze people's habits and feelings and behaviors. Our strategic planner Denise Larson even followed a dozen or so men into the bathroom and watched while they shaved to gather research for our Panasonic shaver campaign.

In the end, we have found that analyzing results from market research is an art, not a science. Rather than take these results as gospel, we consider them part of an overall picture. As Dr. Ona Robinson puts it, we think it's much more important, when engaging in market research, to "tune yourself in to the experience of the group, as opposed to the opinion of the group." We don't just hear their words, we focus on nonverbal cues, on body language, on where people are sitting in relation to one another. Instead of poring over every word, we look to see if participants seem attentive and interested.

After years of watching ideas that exploded and those that fizzled, after decades of experience with market research, we have identified several markers of a Big Bang. Whenever we are considering a series of ideas to present to a client, whenever we are in the midst of consumer testing, we pose the following questions to ourselves in order to identify the one idea with the most potential. Our test isn't foolproof: Occasionally a great idea comes along that fails to meet one of our testing criteria, and we let it go. But we've found that Big Bang ideas obey most if not all of the commandments below.

Here are the questions that we ask every time we do due diligence on a potential Big Bang concept.

Is It Elegantly Simple?

Big Bang ideas are rarely complex. If you are looking for an idea that will stick in people's minds, that is powerful enough to touch their lives, to be imitated, spoofed, and incorporated into everyday jargon, the concept is usually simple. Few people have the time to stop and try to figure out what you're trying to say. Whether the campaign is an idea built around a phrase, a jingle or a picture, a Big Bang advertisement or marketing slogan paints the proverbial thousand words in a moment. "The Quicker Picker-Upper." "Sometimes you feel like a nut, sometimes you don't." "All the news that's fit to print." "Think different." Each of these ideas focuses on one simple concept.

Continental's "Work Hard, Fly Right" campaign, for example, written by KTG creative directors Jack Cardone and Mike Grieco, condensed into four words what Continental needed to tell the world. The airline realized that their target was business travelers who wanted an airline that didn't screw up. That slogan says it all.

James Carville, during Clinton's first campaign, came up with "It's the Economy, Stupid." There were a lot of other problems going on in the country at the time—remember when managed health care first came on the scene?—but he refused to run an ad that didn't focus on that one point. Most political consultants, in fact, will say winning a campaign is all about focusing on one defining issue.

Yet all too often people overlook ideas that could be a Big Bang because the idea doesn't seem "big" enough. A. G. Lafley, CEO of Procter & Gamble told us in a recent meeting, "Every time we have more than two moving parts in something we start to get into trouble. Simpler is so much better. With a new brand, the issue is, 'who are you and what do you do.' For brands that are already out there, the issue is 'try me.' It's just not complicated."

Sometimes advertising or marketing people, in their effort to create something "big," create messages that are confusing. In their desire to create a memorable logo or tagline, they forget that the message must be crystal clear. This concept is exactly what separated the launch of two recent marketing campaigns for wireless services.

Just before the 2002 Super Bowl, a series of ads hit the airwaves talking about something called mLife. "Since nothing came immediately to mind, many of us jumped to the conclusion it must be some new form of life insurance or employee benefits," wrote Rance Crain, editor-in-chief of *Advertising Age*. Eventually, it came out that mLife refers to the wireless cell phones, pagers, and other products offered by AT&T. The ads were so ambiguous that Metropolitan Life Insurance Company immediately filed suit, arguing that "mLife" could easily be confused with "MetLife." The two companies settled the dispute, but the verdict was in. While "mLife" was used by AT&T for a couple of years, the campaign never managed to deliver a message that was instantly crystal clear.

At the same time, Verizon Wireless was running their now famous "Can you hear me now?" ads. They seized on the major issue that bedevils every cell phone user: *It has to work*. Even if it has the capacity to beam you up to Mars, it's worthless if it can't make a connection. The campaign was an immediate success for Verizon Wireless, in large part because the company communicated a crucial point in mere seconds.

The story behind a famous Alka-Seltzer campaign is another illustration of the beauty of simplicity. As Mary Wells Lawrence recounts in her book *A Big Life in Advertising*, she headed up the team that took over the Alka-Seltzer account in the 1960s. Sales were down and Miles Laboratories, the manufacturer of Alka-Seltzer, wanted relief from its dismal bottom line. Wells's people started working on some catchy commercials. But it wasn't until she had a random chat with a doctor employed by Miles that they "hit gold." The doctor demonstrated to Lawrence and her staff the results of a simple discovery: Two Alka-Seltzer tablets are more effective than one. At the time, the directions in the packaging clearly stated that you only needed to take one pill. And every commercial showed a single tablet being dropped into water.

Lawrence and her team quickly went to work. It only took a short time before every commercial for Alka-Seltzer showed two tablets being popped into a glass of water. Miles Laboratories rewrote the instructions, encouraging consumers to take two tablets instead of one. The company created portable two-packs of

"Can you hear me now? Good."℠

THE SIMPLICITY OF VERIZON'S "CAN YOU HEAR ME NOW?" MESSAGE RANG OUT
LOUD AND CLEAR.

Alka-Seltzer and sold them at newsstands, bars, fast-food joints, everywhere. The real Big Bang happened, however, when someone on Lawrence's team came up with "Plop, Plop, Fizz, Fizz." Four short, simple words—and the rest is history.

The campaign went on to become one of the top fifteen advertising campaigns of the century, according to *Advertising Age*. Predictably, sales of Alka-Seltzer virtually doubled. It was a brilliantly simple solution—and it turned the brand around.

Sticking to one clear idea, in fact, is what put the Partnership for a Drug-Free America on the map, says Doria Steedman. Now drug abuse is obviously a subject rife with statistics and medical studies, and many marketers might try to cram as much of this scary info into an ad as possible. In 1987, however, the partnership decided to go with perhaps one of the simplest commercials ever written.

It starts with a man holding an egg. "The actor in the commercial is not a screamer. But he's not pussyfooting around either. He simply holds up an egg and says, 'This is your brain.' Then he cracks it into a hot sizzling pan, and the camera zooms in on the frying egg. He says, 'This is your brain on drugs.'" Steedman says that "it worked because it was simple and disturbing. It was startling." She notes that it is still one of the most highly recognized commercials of all time, resulting in T-shirts, posters, cartoons, spoofs, and more.

It is not always easy to go with the simple solution, however. In fact, it's not always easy to *see* the simple solution. I found this out when, in 1988, Bell Atlantic was sponsoring a special for Barbara Bush's literacy campaign. My friend Chris Clouser, then the vice president of corporate relations and advertising of Bell Atlantic, asked if I could write a commercial. Of course, as with campaigns for so many great causes, we had virtually no budget to work with. "What can we do that costs nothing?" I remember thinking. I ran through various scenarios in my mind: Which celebrity would read Shakespeare for free? How can I cobble together a bunch of compelling images that show how important this

149

COUPLED WITH THE LINE "THIS IS YOUR BRAIN ON DRUGS," THIS IS ONE OF
THE MOST POWERFUL ANTIDRUG METAPHORS OF ALL TIME.

issue is? I began to think that the job was impossible. During one
exasperated moment I remember saying to myself, "Just typeset-
ting the tagline could eat up this budget!" Which of course led our
group to the big "Aha!" Why not do just that—typeset words?
That would be the entire commercial.

The finished spot was merely a scroll of random letters moving
down the screen, underscored with a simple plaintive piano track:

> Flgk ob nst putaahiy snlau.
> Mki ainigh I vpug ct emoem tai.
> Amfn ofa nst putsah ka kukg
> eorf ie k jka kukg. Amfn goa
> tugyg si sbx idtlp
> smqu nb qpqtwrd gycm.

Just when viewers started to feel confused and frustrated, the ad
concluded with the following tagline: "Now you know how millions of American adults feel every time they try to read."

The solution was right under my nose all that time: Text means nothing if you're illiterate. Instead of trying to come up with some overarching theme about literature, instead of spewing statistics about how many adults in America can't read, we let readers experience illiteracy for themselves. In thirty seconds they knew all they needed to know about why they should support the literacy campaign. It was as uncomplicated as that.

When an idea is elegantly simple, it is easy to explain. If you need a thirty-page PowerPoint presentation to explain your idea, you probably don't have a Big Bang. You should be able to lean over to a friend and utter the concept in a sentence. And it is here that research tools such as focus groups can help you. They can let you know if your message is coming across loud and clear.

The beauty of an elegantly simple idea is that it can be boiled down to an icon. Once a brand has been built up over the years, that icon becomes a shortcut for the consumer, creating instant advertising every time you see it: The swoosh for Nike. The bull's-eye for Target. The blue box with a white bow for Tiffany. Just hearing the first seven notes of "When you wish upon a star . . ." triggers a memory of the entire cast of Disney cartoon characters.

Get Therapy

Most researchers seize on what's *said* by people participating in market research forums such as focus groups or ethnographic forays into the street. What's more important is what's *meant*. A good therapist is more tuned in to the emotional content that's in the room as opposed to the verbal content. Because they are expert at reading people's hidden messages, they can help you read the room—not just the verbatim scripts.

Perhaps the perfect example of an icon that stemmed from a brilliantly simple marketing standpoint is Apple's: an apple with a bite taken out of it. Margaret Mark and Carol S. Pearson, in their book *The Hero and the Outlaw,* point out that this ancient symbol "evokes the first act of rebellion in the Garden of Eden, a powerful distillation of the brand's iconoclastic identity." The icon says that Apple users are renegades, people who go against the PC tide. They celebrate all you people who aren't followers, who think different and change the world. It is a logo that both reflects the culture Apple has stayed true to, as well as the brand they have worked so hard to establish.

All of these icons not only make it easier for the consumer to understand your message, points out Mark, who is also a marketing consultant based in Westchester County, New York. They also keep the soul or spirit of the brand alive. "The first generation to market an iconic brand may get it because they were part of its creation, but what about the next generation? Its creators may feel it in their bones, but they need to be able to pass it on," she says. "Whether it's an advertising idea or corporation, you have to use devices like icons or phrases to pass on what the soul of something is." So every new generation can "discover" it for themselves.

Mark spent three months coming up with a verbal expression of the essence of the Ralph Lauren brand. The company felt the need for a succinct articulation of Ralph Lauren's meaning, so that everyone who touches the brand—from a graphic designer to a salesperson—understands the whole aura and romance that's been built around it. She finally came up with a statement that begins with the words, "Ralph Lauren invites you to be part of his romantic journey to wonderful worlds—past and future . . ." It took a long time to articulate the right message, but it was worth the effort, Mark says. "Ralph Lauren could have been marketed in a cold and haughty way. But this has an invitational quality that makes his brands warm and accessible, even to a kid who can only buy a Polo Jeans sweatshirt on sale."

Years ago, my husband Fred and I were asked to write a fundraising song for the United Jewish Appeal-Federation of New York. We needed a simple motif to help us explain a very important message. I knew Fred would come up with a beautiful and memorable song, but I couldn't figure out what the theme and lyric should be. The message we wanted to convey was that Jewish people everywhere needed to recognize their responsibility for keeping their heritage alive. I was searching for a big idea, when the account director casually glanced at their logo and noticed it contained one small but riveting visual detail—a torch. We started to chat about the fact that nearly every Jewish holiday centers around flames: Hannukah menorahs symbolizing the eight days the oil lamps miraculously burned in the Jerusalem temple after the Maccabean victory; Sabbath candles that are lit every Friday night; the Yartzheit candle that burns in remembrance of a loved one who has died. The message, I realized, was right under my nose: *Judaism is an eternal flame that must never die out.*

That small symbolic idea completed the puzzle, and within minutes I found the theme for the film I had been looking for: "Keep the Fire Burning." Fred and I wrote a song to match, and the film went on to raise millions of dollars for the organization.

Is It in the Right Universe?

One of the things people forget in marketing is that we're here to sell things. A lot of advertising is amusing, but it doesn't sell the product. When Taco Bell created their chihuahua icon in the late 1990s, the talking dog was immensely popular. She didn't convince the masses, however, to eat at Taco Bell. When you think about it, few things are less appetizing than a dog selling food. Do you really want to eat food that a dog likes? Dogs will eat anything! As Jorge Mesquita, president of home care/global business unit for Procter & Gamble puts it, "Advertising should be engaging, memorable, and dramatic, but the benefits of the product shouldn't be tangential. You need an idea that is grounded in what the product offers."

Too many marketers waste time and energy on some grandiose

idea to catapult sales and end up with a Big Bang in the wrong universe. The 1996 campaign for Nissan is a good example. That September, Nissan ran an animated ad called "Toys," where a toy soldier falls from the jaws of a dinosaur into the seat of a tiny version of the Z, Nissan's sports car. The creative director was determined to use the Van Halen version of "You Really Got Me," and Nissan ended up giving each member of the band his own new Z car to pay for the privilege.

When it aired, the "Toys" ad was a huge hit in the press, garnering accodales from *USA Today, Entertainment Weekly,* and Oprah Winfrey. It was proclaimed the best ad of the year by *Time* magazine.

And what happened to sales? They fell in September (the month it aired), in October (over 10 percent), in November, and in December, according to the *Wall Street Journal.* Turned out that the Z was being phased out by Nissan at the time—a detail that somehow got ignored. Dealers couldn't believe that Nissan was running an ad that focused on a car that they didn't have on the lot. Besides, what sports-car enthusiast wants to buy a car that looks like a toy?

McDonald's had a similar experience. In the late 1990s they introduced the Arch Deluxe hamburger, which was meant to appeal to adults only. Ads showed kids wrinkling their noses in distaste at the burgers, and Ronald McDonald playing, of all things, golf. The result? Store sales went down. This may have been due to any number of reasons, but one thing is for sure: Those ads alienated the very reason McDonald's exists—kids!

You have to learn to understand what is and what is not important to get across. You must home in on the truly relevant. As unglamorous as it may be, you must reject the temptation to come up with an eye-popping grand strategy instead of focusing on the issue at hand. Shirley Polykoff, the legendary creative muse behind Clairol's early successes with "Does she or doesn't she?" and "Is it true blondes have more fun?," knew exactly whom she was talking to. She always referred to the people buying Clairol hair products as "my ladies." If an ad wasn't relevant to the brand position that appealed to her "ladies," she nixed it.

Eugene Secunda, Ph.D., professor of marketing and media studies at New York University, remembers a terrific example of getting across the right idea to the right people. Years ago, when he was working at J. Walter Thompson, he worked on a recruiting campaign for the U.S. Marine Corps. They came up with "We never promised you a rose garden," in which a drill sargeant is screaming in the face of a recruit. "You might say, 'Who in his right mind would want to have that experience?' " says Secunda. "But there are certain young men who have a need to put themselves in extremely dangerous situations to demonstrate that they are really men, that they can endure the rite of passage to prove you're a man," he explains. And the ad worked because it appealed to exactly those men. "They didn't want some wise-guy sophisticate from the city. They wanted rural, unexposed young men who wouldn't look at their experience skeptically, and would take it at face value," he says. "And it was incredibly successful against this demographic."

Is It Polarizing?

A Big Bang isn't neutral. It forces you to have a point of view. As a result, a Big Bang usually doesn't test well in traditional qualitative research vehicles that look for consensus, such as focus groups. At a time when women were yearning to break the glass ceiling, for example, who ever would have guessed that Martha Stewart would make a bundle mimicking the life of a domestic goddess? As it turned out, however, millions of women were desperate to learn how to be as successful at home as they were at work.

Likewise, if we had relied on focus groups for the AFLAC duck and the Herbal Essences "Totally Organic Experience," they would have ended up on the cutting room floor. Both generated responses

155

ranging from "It's fabulously funny" to "This is insulting." Big Bangs often introduce new ideas, even jarring ideas; as a result they may be initially offputting to some consumers. Charlie Moss, chairman of Moss/Dragoti Advertising in New York, claims that consumers participating in a focus group "may only react to what they understand to be appropriate, thereby killing any idea, as powerful as it might be, that is novel and unique."

Perhaps the best use of focus groups is that they can identify an idea that's polarizing, and thus has the most potential to become a Big Bang. Claire Geier, a strategic planner, recently discovered that when our Herbal Essences ads get a negative response in focus groups, that's not necessarily a bad thing. What matters is that there are also people who simply love the ads. It is often these very iconoclastic ideas that are the ones that catch fire. "Polarization indicates passion and intense feeling," says Geier. "Naturally, some feelings will be negative, but I would be more concerned if responses lacked intensity of feeling." In England, in fact, focus groups are often run to isolate the one idea or product that appeals to a very few "forward-thinking" types. That's the one they seize on as a future success.

Refocus Your Focus Group

It's not the content of what focus group participants say, it's the amount of time they devote to a particular subject that counts. Sometimes women in our focus groups will go on and on about how much they hate an ad, yet they can't stop talking about it. And that's what we want.

Such polarization is a good indicator that your idea will get attention. The last thing you want is an across-the-board lukewarm response. If everyone "sort of" likes it, then it's almost sure to fail.

We recently had an idea for a campaign that generated controversy within the client's own team. It has yet to be tested, but it is a great example of an idea that is so polarizing you can't ignore it.

Lane Bryant, clothier to plus-sized women, asked us to pitch its business. We knew we needed to validate women who didn't conform to the traditional size 4 model. Of course there was no fooling anyone of one thing: Thin will always be in. But, as we started to talk about it, we realized that the tide is changing. Instead of clubbing us over the head with images of anorexic starlets, the media has shown a willingness to back such movies and shows as *My Big Fat Greek Wedding, Less than Perfect, Real Women Have Curves.* Suddenly it seems as if there is a much broader range of what is considered beautiful. Perhaps to an extent this is a post-9/11 phenomenon; marketing consultant Margaret Mark argues that the fertile female body is a comforting image after a stressful time. Before World War II we had the slim-hipped flapper girls of the twenties

Listen for the Word *But*

When you're looking over verbatims from market research interviews, listen for the word *but* in a conversation. Consider the following sentence: "I think that commercial is silly, but it made me laugh." The only words that matter are the ones after the word *but.*

and thirties; postwar pinups were more full-bodied along the lines of Jane Russell, Sophia Loren, and Marilyn Monroe.

As we batted around ideas, we figured that the traditional way to position this company would be to show how fabulous plus-sized women can look in Lane Bryant clothes. But wouldn't it be

throw the world a curve

LANE BRYANT

LANE BRYANT'S CAMPAIGN "THROW THE WORLD A CURVE" CELEBRATES THE NAKED TRUTH—TODAYS AVERAGE WOMAN ISN'T A PERFECT SIZE 4 . . . SHE'S A BIG BEAUTIFUL SIZE 16.

much bolder to tell these women that Lane Bryant sees them as fabulous and appealing? Better yet, why not actually *show* how beautiful these Rubenesque women are? And so art director Stuart Pittman and writer Jill Danenberg came up with a series of elegant black-and-white photographs of nude full-figured women with the tagline "Throw the World a Curve."

Now chances are this won't top the Christian Coalition's list of "best media moments." If the campaign ever runs, these photos will hang in the windows of stores, and you can be sure that plenty of people will march in and ask that they be taken down. When we showed the idea to the client, in fact, several junior people felt that it was too risky. But the minute CEO Dorrit Bern saw the idea, she said, "That's the Big Bang." Yes, it might annoy some people. Yes, it's a clothing store and these ads don't even show a shred of fabric. Yes, nude is always risky. But we think that's precisely what will make it work.

Will It Catch Fire?

One of the best indicators of a Big Bang is whether it can make a good news story. Now, we understand that many corporations are gun-shy of publicity. But as Tricia Kenney, our director of public relations, points out, "either you manage the press, or the press will manage you. If the press wants to do a story, chances are they will do it with or without you, and your point of view may not be represented. People who don't know as much as you do about your company could have a louder voice."

Publicity is one of the fastest routes to a Big Bang. Don't worry about whether the news is good or bad. *Just get covered.* People forget what the content of a story was, but they remember your name. When you don't have a big budget, the press can provide it for you: It is the one tool that can keep any great idea continually in the public mind. Tricia points to the Calvin Klein ads in the eighties and nineties as an example. The company relied heavily on print ads, but "every time they did a print ad, they knew it would get tremendous TV exposure on the news and on the entertainment shows." The company execs knew the ads were so controversial that they "would hit the airwaves."

Ron Shaw, CEO of Pilot Pen, knows that his advertising budget needs to be supplemented by great PR moments. One of our teams, Robin Schwarz and Rob Snyder, recently wrote a spot for Pilot Pen that took advantage of perhaps the bleakest business news story of 2002. The ad opens with a close-up of the hands of a man furiously erasing the writing on page after page after page. As he does this, the visual is accompanied by Chopin's "Funeral March." At the end, a foreboding voiceover says, "What could one Fortune 500 company have done when they were told they could no longer shred their documents? Pilot Pen introduces the first erasable gel ink pen." This Enron parody aired on *The Tonight Show* and got a thumbs-up mention in the *Wall Street Journal*—a real coup for a company that had an advertising budget of less than $10 million.

Shaw took advantage of another PR opportunity one Friday afternoon in 1993 when he got a phone call from his secretary. Yitzhak Rabin and Yasser Arafat were about to sign the Oslo Peace Accord, and the reporters had asked Prime Minister Rabin what kind of pen he would be signing the treaty with. Rabin responded, "I am a man of the people and I keep inexpensive pens in my pocket. Whatever pen is in my pocket tomorrow, that's the one I'll sign with." Shaw had the day off, but his secretary called him just seconds after the treaty was signed. "People keep calling the office to tell us that Rabin used a Pilot pen!" she told him. Shaw raced to his TV and turned on CNN. The historic moment was replayed several times and sure enough, "in one of the close-ups you could read 'PP' on the barrel of the pen," recalls Shaw. "Now the wheels started to turn in my head. What could we do with this that would not be ostentatious or tasteless? How can we boast that our pen was used for this historic occasion?"

It was the marketing opportunity of a lifetime. Shaw eventually decided to buy a full-page ad in twenty-five newspapers across the

GIVING UP SMOKING MADE THIS TOY ONE HOT POTATO!

country. The event happened on a Friday, but he wanted it to be in Monday's paper. His agency was immediately set to work on writing an ad, but he hated all their versions. By chance, his son, commercial director Steve Shaw, called him about an unrelated topic and came up with a brilliant headline: "There's a fine line between war and peace. This one was written with a Pilot Pen." Shaw's publicity people took the story to the Associated Press, who picked it up and ran it in dozens of countries around the world, and it became a PR bonanza.

Mr. Potato Head is another hit that was helped by PR. Years before *Toy Story* made Mr. Potato Head one hot spud, Hasbro issued a statement declaring that in light of all the bad press about smoking, Mr. Potato Head was breaking his decades' old habit and surrendering his pipe to the Surgeon General. At the time, anti-cigarette articles were flooding the media, and millions of people were desperately trying to quit smoking. By capitalizing on a burgeoning trend, Mr. Potato Head made headline news.

Even if you do have money to burn, PR makes a difference. When Michael Jackson's hair caught on fire during the filming of a Pepsi commercial, it was hardly good news. But the incident caused the premiere of that ad to become one of the hottest events of the year worldwide.

Finally, PR breeds PR. Recently Procter & Gamble has changed its whole policy on speaking to the press. They have finally realized that press coverage is a good thing, and are much more open about seeking it. The bottom line is, you're better off taking advantage of PR than not. Once you start getting mentioned in the press, you'll find that reporters keep coming back to you. We get calls all the time because advertising columnists know that we will make their story a top priority. Reporters are just like the rest of us, and won't search any harder than they have to for a story.

Once you've got your Big Bang idea in hand, you still have to sell it to your customer, client, boss, or group. And you have to find a Big Bang way to get a Big Bang sold.

THE THEATER OF

Persuasion
Persuasion
Persuasion
Persuasion

Let's face it. We have become a culture addicted to the show. Whether it's catchy banter during your local weather report, or an epic John Williams theme introducing the NBC evening news, we won't watch it without some razzmatazz. The focus on entertainment permeates every aspect of our culture. Restaurants such as Hard Rock Cafe have capitalized on the thrill of Hollywood. Bowling alleys have disco lights dazzling up their pins. Until recently, you couldn't get into a New York City cab without hearing a message recorded by a celebrity reminding you to put on your seat belt.

In most industries, you win people over by entertaining them. No audience—whether it's a client, the consumer, or the sales or management group of your own company—is going to pay attention merely because you plop something in front of them. How you deliver the information is key. You must serve it up in such a way that it can't be ignored. You must be entertaining.

Last spring, for instance, Coca-Cola debuted its new Vanilla Coke to the public in a carefully orchestrated Norman Rockwell moment. At 10:45 one morning, a delivery truck rolled up to the

Vanilla Bean Café in the cute New England town of Pomfret, Connecticut, and a crowd of school kids (who had the day off) got first dibs on the new soft drink. I once heard Jill Barad, former CEO of Mattel, say that she used to have her department heads sing their quarterly reports. Microsoft recently launched its Tablet PC with appearances by Amy Tan, Rob Lowe, and Stephen Covey. Defense attorneys are famous for their theatrics. Paul Thaler, in his book *The Spectacle: Media and the Making of the O. J. Simpson Story*, points out that showmanship was regularly employed to sway the court of public opinion. "Knowing they were being watched by television, both sides were suspected of elongating the process by contesting legal points regardless of how small or obtuse they may have been," Thaler writes. "Drama, after all, was key."

Last year I asked Whitney Pillsbury, a very talented art director at KTG, to direct a film about our company. I knew that capturing the creative Big Bang ambiance of this company would make for a highly entertaining vehicle for promoting KTG. Whitney ended up producing a fantastic film, *How to Succeed in Advertising, Without Really Crying*, that was well received at the 2002 Director's View Film Festival in Norwalk, Connecticut—Janet Maslin, former film critic and now book critic for the *New York Times*, noted that it was "refreshing and unexpected, charming and funny." The film also won the 2003 DV award for outstanding achievement in Digital Video and it has been a big hit with prospective clients.

A Big Bang, by definition, is a hard sell. When you have a polarizing marketing idea, it's unlikely to sail through the typical decision-making process. Let's face it; a spokes-duck for an insurance company is not, at first glance, a slam dunk. As a result, Big Bang concepts can easily get derailed or outright rejected—especially since they are often vetted by junior people, who tend to accept the familiar and turn down the risky. And the best marketing idea in the world is worthless if no one will buy it.

At KTG, we view every Big Bang presentation as a Broadway show. We view it as a piece of theater that must be blocked out, cast, rehearsed, and refined. Sure, depending on the agenda, some meetings are more theatrical than others. But we know that our clients can easily be distracted by more appealing or more urgent things to do, so we work hard to make sure that they are engaged and entertained while they are enlightened. Our goal is to get our Big Bang idea the standing ovation it deserves. We call this the Theater of Persuasion. It starts the moment you make contact with a potential audience—and, ideally, never ends. Here's how we present our Big Bang ideas.

Set the Stage

Laura Slutsky, who is both a standup comedienne and a successful commercial film director in New York, says, "The audience has to know, from the first moment they see me up on stage, that I'm empowered, I'm a winner. It's the same in business." You must think of your entire interaction with your client as theater. From the moment they enter the door—or you enter theirs—you want to make them feel confident and filled with expectation.

Disney knows this better than anyone. When you work at one of its theme parks, you aren't just an employee. You are a "cast member." Customers are "guests," a crowd is an "audience," a work shift is a "performance," and a uniform is a "costume." From the moment the company's employees get to work to the moment they leave, they live the Disney credo.

This occasionally calls for a little stagecraft. When Quad/Graphics, now the third largest printing company in the country, was starting out in the early 1970s, owner Harry Quadracci would crank up the presses whenever a potential client was coming to visit. He would also artfully stack his rolls of paper so that it appeared the place was stuffed to the gills with waiting jobs—despite the fact that he had almost no work at the time.

Trendspotter Faith Popcorn and her partner, Stuart Pittman (the man who gave me my first freelance job in advertising), who started a New York City ad agency years ago called BrainReserve, have a similar story. At the time the company was tiny enough to fit into Popcorn's studio apartment on the Upper East Side. The smell of her morning coffee was still hanging in the air when the staff of four came to work. One day, the agency got a phone call from the Sally Hansen company, a cosmetics firm that was looking for some marketing help. They asked to come up to the BrainReserve offices.

Few things are less reassuring to a client than saying that you don't have an office. Fortunately, Pittman and Popcorn were members of the Lotos Club, an exclusive arts club in a gorgeous limestone townhouse nearby. Why not temporarily move the office over there? So BrainReserve rented a floor at the Lotos Club for the day, and brought in files, typewriters, and telephones. The client walked in to lavish rooms filled with antiques, priceless Impressionist paintings, and a half dozen or so good but unemployed actor friends pulled in at the last minute to look busy manning all the equipment.

"Our biggest fear," remembers Pittman, "was that someone would ask to make a phone call, because then everyone would find out that none of the phones were actually connected." In the end, the presentation was a success, and the client was impressed enough to hire BrainReserve for one of its projects.

We pulled similar tricks in our early years when we had a much smaller staff. When an important client was coming in for a meeting, I would call for a "West Wing" day at the office. Of course, when we were really busy, there tended to be very few people in the office. Everyone was out shooting commercials or making presentations. But clients didn't understand this. They wanted to see the hustle and bustle, they wanted to sense that they were at the center of the universe, working with *the* hot ad agency.

So I would demand that everyone return to the office, that no one go out to lunch. All of us would then choreograph our moves as if we were performing in an episode from *West Wing,* with the actors purposefully walking in front of the camera and spinning off in several different directions at once. I'd tell everyone, "I want all the computers turned on—I don't care if you're looking at your stock portfolios." As I would walk the client from the foyer to my office, I'd say, "I'd love to introduce you to everyone, but we're all so busy." I'd have people crossing my path, and clusters of people would look up and say, "Oh, hi, can't talk!" Then, when the client would leave, everyone would scurry back to work and the office would empty out again.

Rehearse 'til You Drop

Most people benefit from a simple run-through the night before a presentation, but our dress rehearsals are so exhausting that they would make Actors' Equity go on strike. I have a nearly obsessive insistence on ensuring that every detail of a presentation is thought out. If it doesn't flow just right, you won't get the laugh, or the gasp or the teary eyes. It's all in the timing and the material.

Every point you make needs to flow logically and effortlessly to the next one. This means rolling up your sleeves and getting

Go Low-Tech

A bad idea is bad no matter how you dress it up. Sometimes technological pyrotechnics allow us to masquerade mediocre thinking. But they can never make up for a bad idea. Technology soaks up time, energy, and money that should be redirected into actual creative thinking. Going low-tech forces you to be closer to the actual ideas. Remember: 21 gigaflops of processing power won't turn a half-baked idea into a Big Bang—or even a mini bang.

bogged down in minutiae. When we presented our Blimpie campaign, for example, I spent almost an hour working with the art director on exactly where he should hold the storyboards.

It helps to take a page from the world of show business, where ripping things up at the last minute is a way of life. A number of years ago my husband, Fred Thaler, an award-winning Broadway and movie composer/arranger, was the musical director for *Platinum*, starring Alexis Smith. Before it went to Broadway, it was performed in theaters around the country to test the waters and to fine-tune the performance. "When we were on the road, the director would constantly be reblocking scenes, rewriting dialogue, and adding or eliminating songs or dances. You could be in Boston one night with one show, and then have it seriously revamped by the time you performed it in Philly a week later. One choreographed change, one new lyric, might very well mean I'd have to completely restructure an orchestral arrangement. We sweated every detail, but by the time it reached Broadway, we had standing ovation audiences every night."

If you just throw something together at the last minute, no matter how good the pieces are, everyone in the room will end up embarrassed, and your client will just spend the time figuring out how to avoid you in the future. It's not a great career builder. "Lack of rehearsal is by far the most common mistake business presenters make," says a report in the *Harvard Management Communication Letter* on how to make a presentation. " 'I'll just wing it' are the four saddest words in the business lexicon."

Burt Manning, former CEO of J. Walter Thompson, told me a story that illustrates this perfectly. When J. Walter Thompson was bought by WPP, now the world's leading advertising and marketing services group, several longtime Thompson clients around the globe decided it would make good sense to review their agencies.

One was the Ford Motor Company group in Brazil. The meeting was important enough for Ford to fly several top executives from Dearborn down to São Paolo. Manning also flew down to Brazil, with the idea that he could help pull together and rehearse

JWT's presentation—a comprehensive look at the Brazilian car market. Manning, however, arrived too late for any adjustments, too late to look at a dress rehearsal, too late to do anything but sit in the audience with the client and hope.

Fifteen minutes into the presentation, Manning knew it was over. Why? Not because the wrong guy was at center stage. The man chosen to make the heart of the presentation was the key man on the business, a seasoned Brazilian car guy. The only one, Manning was told later, knowledgeable enough to make such a presentation.

The only problem was that the importance of this meeting—and the lack of a run-through—completely unnerved him. He turned his back to the client. Then, in a monotone so low it was barely audible, he proceeded to read directly from his charts—every word, every number. And there were *thousands* of them. One of the Ford clients very politely requested that he speak a little louder. That made him even more nervous.

If JWT's work was good, nobody in the audience could possibly have known it. Manning called it the most agonizing two hours he had ever spent in the advertising business.

With their confidence in JWT Brazil shattered, Ford moved the business. Manning later told us that just one thorough, day-long dress rehearsal—normal for a presentation this important—would have made all the difference. The presentation would have been cut by thirty minutes. The presenter would have been coached, encouraged, rehearsed. And possibly the agency would have kept the business.

The night before you present a Big Bang idea to your boss, your client, or your sales force, it's important to get your team riled into a mildly agitated state. Nothing is more dangerous than thinking that a presentation will be a piece of cake. Complacency sets in, people get overly confident, preparation slips, and inevitably, the show is a failure. You want everyone pumped with adrenaline, totally focused and on heightened alert.

Nervous energy, in fact, is what enables people to present polarizing, disruptive—and occasionally outlandish—ideas. KTG writers Hal Friedman and Robin Schwarz once came up with a hilarious idea for a local gas company, entitled "We give you gas." Only adrenaline, remembers Friedman, could propel him to "go into a huge board room so pristine we weren't allowed to bring in cups of water, stand in front of a group of fourteen perfectly dressed, solemn, and attentive board members assembled in proper pecking order, and present a campaign of fart jokes."

Finally, never assume your equipment is going to work. We have seen pitches lost due to technical fiascos: A faulty television monitor that turned dazzling Clairol auburn tresses into lime green heads, a set of bad speakers that made a rousing anthem sound like a chorus of angry ants, and the meeting where we were only able to click the PowerPoint slides backward. Imagine ending a new business pitch with "Introduction," and you'll get an idea of how far south a meeting can go.

By the way, as you put together the pieces of your presentation, try to use PowerPoint sparingly. Of course PowerPoint is useful and even crucial for certain presentations. But it is also dehumanizing. Ian Parker, in *The New Yorker*, wrote that PowerPoint has created a world where people present to one another rather than have a lively discussion of the issue at hand. Former army secretary Louis Caldera complained to the *Wall Street Journal* about the overuse of PowerPoint, claiming that "people are not listening to us, because they are spending so much time trying to understand these incredibly complex slides."

Think of it this way: Every second your audience is looking at a demographics chart is one more second they have their eyes off of you—a real, live person. We've been in presentations where the clients never really got to see us at all, with the lights dimmed, and endless screens flipping by. We were in a new business meeting a few months ago, where the prospective client watched one of our account executives, who, in turn, was mesmerized by her own PowerPoint display. She never once made eye contact with the client. Guess how that new pitch turned out? Be prepared to throw away those trusty bullet points and put in some quality face time with your prospective partners.

Know Your Audience

Before you walk into a meeting, make sure you do your homework. You need to find out as much as you can about the client, his idiosyncracies, tastes, and, especially, his current worries. Otherwise, even the best marketing idea in the world won't fly.

Let me give you an example: When Chris Clouser, at the time a top executive of Northwest Airlines, was looking for a new ad agency, he met with a team to hear their ideas for a new marketing campaign. The team walked in the door, eager and confident, and

Assume Nothing

Make sure you have a cheat sheet on everyone in the room, including your colleagues who work in another office. A former coworker at J. Walter Thompson learned this the hard way. Several years back she was asked to present a campaign to the Japanese Kodak team that had just arrived from Tokyo. She walked in a minute late and missed the introductions—a crucial mistake. She proceeded to present the entire campaign to one man, who kept smiling and nodding throughout the whole presentation. After the meeting, she was informed that she had just presented the campaign to her colleague, the J. Walter Thompson Tokyo account executive. The real client had been in back of her the whole time, craning his neck to see the boards. The Japanese client had simply been too polite to correct her.

proceeded to fill the room with speakers. Northwest, they said, needs to be positioned as a strong and powerful airline, with clout and cachet, much bigger than its regional-sounding name would suggest. So every commercial should start with a huge roar, the loudest booming takeoff sound you can imagine, to demonstrate the sheer power of this expansive company. To illustrate their point, the team peppered their presentation with a Surround Sound *roar!* emanating from all the speakers.

Clouser knew in an instant that these people had not done their homework. Had this creative team done a cursory news search of recent Northwest history, they would have discovered that the airline was in the middle of a nasty lawsuit in their hometown of Minneapolis. Why? Their jets were too loud, and residents were complaining of noise pollution. A loud roar was the very *last* thing that Northwest wanted to bring to the consumer's attention. The agency, needless to say, didn't land the business.

I'm sorry to say that we have a similar story from our archives. If we had spent a little bit more time getting to know our client, we could have avoided losing a nice piece of business.

Udder Disaster

We were once asked by a client to explore how we could help them advertise a whole line of special milk products. Milk is a commodity item, which means that most people just buy the cheapest kind they can find. This company wanted us to come up with a strategy to convince consumers to pay extra for their value-added items. It was a simple request.

We decided, however, to come up with a strategy for how the company could market nearly every dairy product they own, from lactose-free milk to ice cream. We are so creative, we thought to ourselves, why can't we help this company reposition its entire product line? So we set to work coming up with a whole new marketing campaign. In particular, we zeroed in on the packaging, which featured a pleasant if innocuous design. *That* doesn't say great-tasting milk, we said to ourselves. But you know what does? Cows. Lots of 'em. KTG did a total makeover of the milk cartons, replacing their logo with the warm, friendly face of a cow. The cow symbolized freshness, just-milked flavor, everything you'd want your kids to wash down an Oreo with.

The day of the meeting we walked in and sat down. "I know you wanted us to think just about this one line of products," I said to the client. "But we have a great idea. We think you could reposition your entire marketing strategy for every dairy product that you sell. To start with, we think you need a new design for your cartons." And with a flourish, I unveiled a board with our friendly cow gazing out at the senior guy at the company.

Wrong moooove. The client instantly stood up and informed us in no uncertain terms that he would never allow a cow on one of his dairy products. Then he abruptly left the room to get a "phone call." That's when his staff apologetically told us that this guy had designed the cartons himself.

In a vain attempt to salvage the meeting, we immediately backpedaled, agreeing that design was not our forte and we had no business going there. "We do know how to make commercials, though," I remember saying, "and we'd love to show you what we've come up with." Unfortunately, without a Plan B in our pocket (see Chapter 9), we had to show them the only storyboards we had with us. They featured, you guessed it, cows. But not just cows. Talking cows, talking cows walking out of subways, talking cows walking down the street, talking cows going into houses . . . Needless to say, the meeting didn't end with a round of high fives. Lesson learned: Do your homework.

Have a Warm-up Act

Just like a comic doing a warm-up for the main attraction, you have to get the audience to like you first. As Dr. Ilene Cohen, clinical associate professor of psychology at NYU Medical School, says, "In therapy, just like marketing, you have to hook people on an emotional level first before they will be receptive to a rational discussion or the exchange of information." Getting people into a receptive mood is especially important for a Big Bang idea. Dr. Cohen elaborates on that principle: "When dealing with situations of cognitive dissonance—that is, trying to present an idea that is too far away from where the patient's beliefs currently are—you need to get them to where you want gradually so they don't completely reject the idea you are trying to introduce. So first you must create trust."

Charlotte Beers, until recently the Bush administration's undersecretary of state for public diplomacy and public affairs, used a similar trick years ago when she was an advertising executive pitching the Sears business. Sears was then a store known primarily for selling typical guy stuff like power tools and radial tires. When she walked into the meeting, she knew that because she was a woman most of the people there would instantly dismiss her. She saw one thought written all over the Sears men's faces: What can *she* do for us? Beers had only a few minutes to allay their fears and convince them that she could handle the account.

As she began her presentation, she pulled out a power drill and put it on the table. She continued to talk about her marketing concepts while she casually took the drill apart and put it back together. Not once did she talk about the drill or even refer to it. It was an audacious move, but it sent a powerful message: I may be a woman, but I know your business inside out. So listen up.

She won the account.

Of course, it's crucial to maintain a good rapport at all times with your client. Jack Cardone and Mike Grieco, one of our creative teams, created Continental's famous "Work Hard, Fly Right" campaign: "A lot of airlines promise you the stars. How about getting your luggage back?" and "The first rule in building a better airline: Don't look to other airlines for inspiration." During one of their meetings with Continental—after the airline had won its fifth J. D.

Power Award for customer satisfaction—the creative team presented a Continental ad with the words "It's official. We don't suck." Everyone in the room cracked up. Cardone and Grieco knew the ad would never see the light of day, but they also knew it would reassure the Continental folks that they understood the airline's ethos.

Take Down the House

When it comes to the actual presentation, look for every opportunity to put on a showstopper. As with a theatrical performance, every moment has to be orchestrated so that there isn't a second of dead space. "All presentations should be entertaining," says Maurice Lévy of Publicis Groupe, "because the presentation of an ad campaign is in itself a reward for the management."

The energy level must be set at full throttle from the very beginning, and kept up throughout the meeting. If Nathan Lane could do eight performances a week playing Max Bialystock in *The Producers*, surely you can hang in there for one short presentation. Back in my previous life, when I was in the touring company for *Stop the World—I Want to Get Off*, I did the show countless times. I discovered that the real talent of actors is not just that they can perform, but that they can do it day in and day out, week after week, and make it fresh and exciting each time. You must remember, as most actors do, that while you may have done this dozens of times before, it will always be brand-new to your audience.

It helps to remind everyone on your staff to be constantly focused on the speaker, even if it's someone who's presenting the same old spiel about your company that you've been hearing for a year and a half. Think this sounds unnecessarily picayune? Next time you go to the opera, check out the supernumeraries—the guys holding the spears while the tenor delivers his aria. They never sing a note, but their attention to the soloist is unwavering. They hear this guy sing seventy performances a year, yet every trill seems to fill them with awe and rapture. Likewise, *you can't look interested enough in your own business.* Remember, you are on stage and have a part to play. If you look mesmerized, everyone else in the room will think they should be too.

Which brings us to our next point. Not everyone is a great presenter. There is a reason why Meryl Streep is a star and the rest of us were shrubs in the third-grade play. So we assign appropriate roles to the members of our team. Robin is commanding when presenting our credentials, so she does the talking during this part of the meeting. Denise Larson, our strategic planner, is funny and quick on her feet, and can make a demographic chart sound like a script for a Jay Leno opening monologue.

When it comes to winning the business, you need to forget about being fair. No matter who came up with the work, no matter who is the most senior person on the account, the best actor gets to present the work. Some people (and this may even include you) may be asked to be quiet for the meeting. It can be difficult for team members to accept that they won't be presenting their work, but you must help them to understand that you all have one goal in mind: Sell the idea.

With the right interplay among your team members, you create a chemistry that inspires confidence and makes each member of your team more attractive. In just about every pitch we've been in, people have come up to us afterward to say, "You guys really seem to like each other." With a couple of clients, that chemistry has even clinched the deal.

Of course, throughout any meeting, a client may interrupt the rhythm of your show with a glib comment or an offhand joke. Sometimes these funny parlays are simply meant to melt the ice. But they can also be a test to see if you have the street smarts and savvy to think on your feet and come up with quick marketing solutions. Like a heckler in a standup club, your client may really be asking "How good are you?" It never hurts to have a comeback to show just how graceful and clever a partner you can be.

Most marketing meetings hit a low point when you need to present material that everybody in the room is already familiar with. This can happen when you give an overview of your client's competitive environment, for example, to reassure them that you understand their business. Or you need to present background information that lays the groundwork for your Big Bang idea. Obviously, this isn't terribly interesting to most people in the room. This is the point at most meetings, in fact, when you're liable to see a rash of bent heads, the telltale sign of a BlackBerry addict answering his email.

If you put a little show biz in your act, however, you can sail through this often mundane material. When we went to pitch Midas, for example, we decided to present a funny video in lieu of a boring analysis of the competition. David Mester, a brilliant film editor at The Blue Rock Editing Company in New York City, came up with a fictional company called "Genericorp," which promised to make sure your product blends in with the rest. Based on that, he created a video that took a satiric stab at all the indistinguishable car-repair ads out there, turning a negative point into a funny

Watch for the Hook
You need to be aware when you're getting the hook—when your idea or presentation just isn't working. Nonverbal cues—a glance at a watch, a stifled yawn—can tell you more about what a client really feels than anything he or she says. Always have a backup plan, a second script, if the meeting is heading off course. And just like Leno, when a joke falls flat on the audience, admit that you laid an egg and crack a few jokes to cut the silence.

sixty-second film. The script, accompanied by tired-looking clips and hackneyed stock music, read as follows:

> Genericorp proudly presents: Advertising your automotive repair shop!
>
> Rule #1: Happy mechanics! Show your mechanic having fun—and don't just show them working on cars. Show them working on cars in *snappy* uniforms!
>
> Rule #2: Lots of numbers! [revealing shot after shot of discount prices] Yes, nothing engages the viewer more than a lot of numbers! Especially ones ending in 95!
>
> *Rule #3:* Smiling customers! Yes, there's nothing more truthful than the broad, satisfied smile customers are always wearing when leaving their local automotive repair shop!
>
> By following this simple equation, you can advertise *your* auto repair shop! And remember: If it's not Genericorp, *it's not the same!*

It was so funny and effective that we have presented a Genericorp video to nearly every new client since. Instead of just talking to our clients ad nauseum about how similar all the advertising is in their category, we let these videos make the point much more dramatically, memorably, and effectively.

Even presenting a brand strategy, which is traditionally done with slides and charts and is about as exciting as watching paint dry, can be an opportunity for theater. When we pitched the Panasonic men's shaver business a couple of years ago, for instance, we knew that our strategic platform, "Shaving Sucks," could come across as obnoxious. While this strategic platform wasn't new to Panasonic, they had nonetheless spent years advertising the fact that their shaver made for a truly enjoyable shaving experience. Truth be known, being the world's fastest shaver did make this irritating ritual "suck less" than competitive brands, but the case was closed. Shaving is a chore.

We knew that if we didn't present this rather negative positioning in a lighthearted way, our client might never get past the first PowerPoint slide. So I decided to present our strategy, not in words, but in song.

I casually lifted my forty-pound Yamaha electric piano onto my lap, and with a chorus of eight KTG male employees backing me up, sang our positioning statement to a tune I had hammered out the night before:

> *Shaving sucks, shaving sucks, like a Band-Aid*
> *getting stuck*
> *Why does half the human race, tear the hair out*
> *of its face?*
> *Shaving sucks, shaving sucks, I would give a*
> *million bucks*
> *To have skin like Cleopatra, but what cologne*
> *would I use aftah?*
>
> *Shaving sucks, shaving sucks, it's just dumb*
> *genetic luck*
> *I'm so perfect in other manly ways,*
> *I'll put the toilet seat down for ya,*
> *Take the garbage from the foyah,*
> *But please don't make me ever shave!*

The Panasonic client was immediately taken with our mini-musical. They later told us that our presentation revealed that we had the talent and energy to translate our thinking into great creative moments. Our performance put us on the short list of contenders and persuaded Panasonic to take a close look at our proposed campaign materials. Eventually we were awarded the business.

Finally, it's crucial, in any presentation, to keep the best for last. As in any play or movie, as soon as you guess the ending, you lose interest. Likewise, you should never reveal your Big Bang idea until the end. Your goal should be to keep the suspense up, and to keep the audience on the edge of its seat, no matter how padded the leather cushions are. We never hand out presentation booklets, scripts, or anything that will distract the client, or let them race ahead to the finale before the closing scene. We want them to *experience* our Big Bang idea, not read about it in bullet points. As Randi Dorman, group director of the New York City–based brand-consulting company Interbrand says, "You need to take them on the same journey that you've gone through, from going through the analysis to the final discovery."

As you finally unveil your brilliant insight, you can do one of two things: You can tell them how brilliant and creative you are. Or you can *be* brilliant and creative. It's like comedy. I can either say to you that Robin Williams is one of the funniest people alive, or I can tell you the wet-burkha-contest joke from his recent post-Taliban routine. The jokes are the proof in the pudding.

Come Back with an Encore

Every meeting with a prospective client should be followed through. You want to communicate just how passionately you feel about their business. As in any theatrical presentation, the encore will be your last impression, which is why it's meant to be a show-stopper. The recent revival of *The Music Man*, brilliantly choreographed by Susan Stroman, ended each performance with the entire cast playing "Seventy-Six Trombones!" on their own individual trombones.

We work hard at coming up with attention-grabbing encores. When we pitched the Coldwell Banker business, America's largest realtor for upscale homes, we knew we were up against the biggest agencies in the country: J. Walter Thompson, Grey Advertising, and McCann-Erikson WorldWide, to name a few. Although our commercial idea featured a tango jingle that my husband, Fred Thaler, composed, and that I unabashedly sang (and danced) at the meeting, we knew we needed to put on another song and dance before they made their final agency decision the following week.

Robin came up with a brilliant idea. The company is head-quartered in Parsippany, New Jersey, only about forty minutes from Manhattan, so we figured they were all readers of the *New York Times*. It was a no-brainer to figure out which section a real estate agent would open to first. Just a few days after our final meeting, our Coldwell Banker clients scanning the real estate ads of the *Times* suddenly saw the following:

GREAT NEW HOME

JUST 50 MINUTES FROM DOWNTOWN PARSIPPANY

Sunny, bright idea factory with unusual flair, style and more Big Bang for your buck. Step up to a world in which your imagination (and business) can soar. Warm, welcoming atmosphere. Convenient Midtown location. Fully stocked refrigerator.

Call the Kaplan Thaler Group.

Ask for Linda.

They answered the ad, by calling me up and awarding us the business.

Once you sell your Big Bang idea, you might feel as if you're done. Mission accomplished. The fact is, however, your most important work is still ahead of you. Everything you've done up to this point lives or dies in how you execute it. And it all comes down to the *details*.

Sweat

THE SMALL STUFF

Creating a Big Bang idea is a long way from actually creating a Big Bang. An idea is not a product or marketing campaign. It is simply the *possibility* of something explosive, a concept yet to be realized. The ability to come up with terrific ideas is invaluable—we have, after all, devoted the previous chapters to doing just that—but it is only half the job. A Big Bang idea must then be executed with flawless, unwavering attention to detail in order to become a Big Bang in the marketplace.

Everyone genuflects at the artists and designers whose hallmarks can be found in the details. The difference between a little black dress by Armani and the sixty-nine-dollar knock-off at Filene's Basement may all be in the stitching, but you'll look like a million bucks in one, and a hooker in another. We believe that marketing is no different. How a concept is executed can make or break a marketing campaign. As former CEO and best-selling authors Larry Bossidy and Ram Charan state in *Execution: The Discipline of Getting Things Done*, "Execution has to be a part of a company's strategy and its goals. It is the missing link between aspirations and results." Leaders who ignore details are "building houses without foundations."

The entire senior management team at KTG has a healthy obsession with details. It stems from years of experience working on successful—and some unsuccessful—campaigns. We value the person who finesses the audio mix, for example, as much as the one who wrote the song. After all, what good is a great spot if no one can hear it? We believe in an ensemble work ethic as we work on a marketing campaign, and set the tone by carefully scrutinizing every step of the process. It's only when everyone in the company is sweating the small stuff that your Big Bang idea doesn't get lost in the minutiae.

Here's how we make sure every detail is in place.

Become a Micromanager

To "micromanage a project" is to commit a dreaded, politically incorrect, anti-empowering sin. Universally disdained by corporate cultures from New York to New Zealand, it is a common belief that micromanagers inhibit creative thinking and short-circuit employee responsibility. Moreover, common wisdom has it that micromanagers get bogged down in all the petty little details better left to junior staffers, and lose sight of the big picture. *This is perhaps the biggest myth among marketing executives.* The fact is that it is all those petty little details that determine whether you successfully create a Big Bang that explodes into the culture.

Most senior executives like to parade as big-picture folks, flaunting the notion that strategy requires genius—their genius—and that execution is just about getting things done. Consequently, the message they communicate to their employees is that moving up the ladder means thinking in broad, sweeping strokes, leaving the detail work to underlings. Such grunt work isn't worthy of their time or expertise. Well, to put it bluntly, we categorically disagree.

Imagine impressionist artist Georges Seurat drawing an outline for *A Sunday Afternoon on the Island of La Grande Jatte* and then leaving it to his students to fill in the colored dots. It is unlikely that the picture that resulted would be great art. Yet this is the kind of thinking done by marketing executives at too many companies. As Bossidy and Charan point out in *Execution*, "Intelligent, articulate conceptualizers don't necessarily understand how to execute. Many don't realize what needs to be done to convert a vision into specific tasks."

Pantene, now the world's most popular shampoo, owes much of its success in the 1990s to the details of how the commercials were shot. P&G executive Rob Matteucci says this campaign turned Pantene into a $1.6 billion business. The ads were primarily a stupendous series of beautiful hair filmed in a variety of surprising ways: tied in knots, unleashed before the camera, pulled across the back of a sofa. "How the hair was shot was crucial," said Matteucci. "Trust me, it's an art. And if it had been the slightest bit off, it would not have worked. Unless you have executional details like this that wow people and complete the story, you're going to miss your Big Bang."

Toys "R" Us recently decided to revive Geoffrey the Giraffe as its spokescreature. Cheryl Berman, the chief creative director at Leo Burnett USA, who runs the account, remembers faxing Toys "R" Us CEO John Eyler pictures of Geoffrey's hair, smile, and expression. Eyler knew that there was a lot riding on this image, says Berman. The giraffe needed to seem real and trustworthy, yet still have a good sense of humor, and Eyler wanted to make sure every detail was right.

An eye for detail, in fact, has been the signature of so many of our great marketing geniuses. Bill Bernbach, the famous creator of Volkswagon's "Think Small" concept and Life cereal's "Mikey" campaign, was famous for looking at, say, a three-phrase block of copy and snapping, "Make it a half-line shorter." A. G. Lafley, the CEO of Procter & Gamble, knows that a brand can live or die depending on seemingly inconsequential details. He recently flew over to Greece, and while there stopped at a household appliance store. The company's Swiffer mop was not selling and he wanted to know why. After one quick waltz down the aisle, Lafley spotted the reason: the Swiffer mop was tucked away in the back where no one could see it. After a brief chat with the store owner, Lafley arranged for the mop to be displayed standing up, where customers couldn't miss it. Some might say that's micromanaging. We say that this is a big part of the reason that Procter & Gamble's stock has skyrocketed from $57 a share when Lafley took over to about $90 today. The lesson: You're never too big to think small.

Let a Detail Ignite the Fuse

When you micromanage, you create details that have the ability to spark a consumer reaction and grab attention. We call this a defining moment, when a simple element pops up that captures the essence of your idea in an imaginative way. After one hilarious episode of *Seinfeld*, for example, when Jerry and company repeatedly abbreviated their conversations with the phrase "yada, yada, yada," it became part of our cultural jargon. As with other phrases—"Show me the money," "Frankly, my dear, I don't give a damn," "Houston, we've got a problem"—it was a simple phrase that instantly crystalized the show. In the consumer's mind, "yada, yada, yada" became the shortcut to the brand.

Such defining moments are rarely in the original concept or marketing plan. All too often the detail that captures the public's eye is unearthed during the execution process, *after* the concept has been created and approved. In fact, these defining moments are often just random suggestions during the production process. Here's an example. In 1986, Tom Bodett, the famous spokesperson for Motel 6, was recording a batch of radio ads created by The Richards Group ad agency in Dallas. The copywriting team had come up with several scripts filled with downhome humor, and Bodett's folksy voice was perfect for pitching this no-frills chain. All was going smoothly until one script ended with a few seconds remaining on the tape. Bodett, to fill the dead air, quickly ad-libbed, "We'll leave the light on for you."

That folksy line summed up the coziness of the brand and, you could argue, put Motel 6 on the map. It became the very signature of the company. The chain grew from around 400 motels to over 800 today and is now one of the leading budget chains in the country. The campaign has won more than 150 awards, including eight Clios, and launched an entire career for Bodett himself.

Great creative moments like this can be easily missed if the right people aren't around to notice them. If we weren't obsessed with the painstaking process of execution, we would never have identified the crucial moment when the AFLAC duck "got" his personality. We knew, going into production for "Park Bench," the first AFLAC commercial featuring two coworkers on a lunch break, that the duck was a great idea. We already had enough test results to indicate that the spot would help AFLAC become better known.

THE KICKER THAT CRYSTALLIZED THE AFLAC DUCK'S FEISTY PERSONA.

Then the director, Tom Rouston, came up with a suggestion. If the guys are eating sandwiches, he said, why doesn't one of them absentmindedly throw a crumb at the duck? Then, at the end, the AFLAC duck can defiantly kick a crumb back at them.

The minute we heard it, we knew that we had the pivotal moment of the campaign. Right there, with the duck's defiant kick, his entire personality was formed, and the critical leverage point of the advertising was crystallized: The duck has an important piece of information that he wants to share and he's furious that no one's listening. It turned the duck from a sweet, feathered mascot to a gutsy critter with attitude. The ending rounded out the duck's personality and gave the campaign a bit of edgy humor. It also became the guidepost for what every other commercial has to have: a moment when the duck groans, kicks, squawks in ornery frustration.

Now, if we were the sort of company that left the execution of our commercials to junior staff members, that ending might never have happened. Rouston could have made his suggestion, and a junior executive could easily have nixed the idea, fearful of deviating from the approved script. As it was, we had Tom Amico and Eric David, a terrific senior team on the job, who immediately recognized that this detail was the sort that could turn their good idea into a great idea. Into, in fact, a Big Bang.

Plenty of other great marketing campaigns have been launched by a detail that happened after all the contracts were signed. "Steven," the teen heartthrob who convinced people across the country to get a Dell, wasn't much of a star when the campaign first launched in 2000. Then Dell switched their account to advertising agency DDB/Chicago. The DDB folks decided to add a short phrase, "Dude, you're gettin' a Dell." *Bingo*. That moment crystallized what the company wanted to get across: Dell is cool. The phrase said, in essence, that you're not just getting any old computer, you're getting the top of the line, el primo hardware. You're getting something your friends will be jealous of, the teenager's first choice. And the alliteration of "Dude, you're getting a Dell" makes it easy to remember. "Dude, you're getting a Hewlett-Packard" wouldn't cut it.

"Steven" became a celebrity, hawking a line of Dude-wear on his website. The campaign has been one of the most successful in advertising, according to *BrandWeek* magazine. It is one of the reasons Dell's sales jumped 18 percent in the second quarter of 2002, while the rest of the industry's shrank 4 percent.

When Charlie Moss was at Wells, Rich, Greene in the 1970s, his team came up with the concept "I Love New York." Everyone adored it, because the slogan perfectly captured the national sentiment at the time: There really is no place like New York—even if it did have a garbage strike and a budget deficit the size of the gross national product of most small nations. It was a campaign that could help to turn the city around.

Then Milton Glaser, the famous graphic designer, agreed to create some posters for New York State, based on the campaign. He came over to the Wells, Rich, Greene offices with a batch of posters. "While we were oohing and aahing over them," recounts Mary Wells Lawrence (Moss's boss at the time) in *A Big Life in Advertising,* "he pulled a piece of paper out of his pocket and said 'I like this, what do you think?' " He showed them the line scribbled on the piece of paper, "I ♥ New York."

And in that moment, Moss's campaign turned into a Big Bang. By changing the word to a symbol, the sentence became participatory. Rather than something that was just handed to you, it engaged you; you had to work to read it. It was the proverbial picture that said a thousand words: That particular heart symbol communicates a very specific happy-go-lucky, pie-eyed, Valentine's Day kind of love. It was so contagious, says Lawrence, that "half the world copied it, substituting the name of their country or city or hamburger stand for 'New York.'"

Learn to Procrastinate

Great defining moments don't happen on cue. In fact, they often come to light at the last possible minute, long after you were supposed to be finished. That's why we advocate procrastination during the execution process, as contradictory as it sounds. You must always go into the execution of every marketing campaign with the idea that something bigger may explode. While your original idea may be fabulous, you should always leave open the possibility for more detail or other improvement. Rather than locking yourself in prematurely, you need to establish a flexible mind-set that allows for something better to come along. By putting off finalizing the project, you increase the chances that some detail that ignites a Bang will materialize.

Creative director Greg Weinschenker and I were shooting a commercial for Burger King during my J. Walter Thompson days. We had written a commercial promoting Burger King's new salads, which were served either on a platter or in a pita bread. The idea was to interview several people and ask them the question, "Do you want a platter or a pita?" We got enough funny responses to make a charming commercial. But we insisted on shooting more folks to see if we could get something better. We were just about to wrap things up, when we interviewed a guy who had no idea what a pita was. When we asked him if he wanted a platter or a pita, he responded, "Peter? He's a nice guy." That was it, the moment we were looking for. It turned out to be the detail that catapulted the campaign into popular culture. The "Peter" line hit the comedy clubs, and even ended up in a late-night talk show opening monolog.

Phil Dusenberry recently reminded us of a story about filming a Pepsi commercial. A few years back, his team wrote an ad entitled "Security Camera." It was shot in grainy black and white, featuring a Coke salesman stocking the soda case in a deli. As he finishes up, he wipes the glass door clean and notices the adjoining Pepsi case. Looking around furtively, he reaches in and swipes a

Pepsi. Suddenly he looks up and notices the security camera recording his every move. The screen goes black.

During the shooting, the BBDO team, under the leadership of Ted Sann, BBDO New York's chief creative officer, realized that the ending lacked pizzazz. In fact, it might make the whole ad fizzle; while it was a funny concept, a dull ending would dilute the power of the joke. So they came up with a new ending: When the Coke guy pulls out his Pepsi, the entire case of cans comes cascading out onto the floor. This Niagara Falls of cans isn't just recorded on the security camera, but also immediately attracts the attention of every person in the store.

That ending did two things: It made you laugh, and it contained the essence of the commercial's message—Look who's drinking a Pepsi! While the concept was a good idea in the first place, says Dusenberry, "that one touch made all the difference." The commercial debuted on the Super Bowl and was voted the number one Super Bowl spot in a *USA Today* survey.

I had a similar experience when I was group creative director at J. Walter Thompson. Naomi Norman, senior copywriter, had written a campaign for Nestlé Toll House called "Please don't eat all the morsels." The visuals showed moms and kids, husbands and wives having a lot of fun making chocolate chip cookies. While they were baking, however, they kept eating the chocolate chips, until all they were left with was a batch of bland cookies.

When we got to the studio to record the song for the commercials, however, the humor of the spot just wasn't coming through. The catchy jingle, composed by Fred Thaler, was sung in a very cute, but expected way, and the vocal sounded as vanilla and bland as those chipless cookies. So we asked the singer to start fooling around with different vocal styles, including country, rock, and Broadway. On a whim, our singer started suddenly performing the jingle with an overblown operatic voice. This *basso profundo* Wagnerian interpretation had everyone in the studio absolutely hysterical.

Although he did this as a joke, I immediately saw how funny the juxtaposition of a pompous aria with an innocent Toll House cookie was. This operatic delivery was the detail that could make people pay attention. It conveyed exactly the right note of smug silliness that infects everyone who sneaks the last chocolate chip. And so we went with it. The campaign did phenomenally well.

Don't Let a Detail Derail the Bang

As with the Big Bang that created the universe, if one tiny particle is out of place in your marketing Big Bang, you could end up with a lot of nothing. It doesn't take but one false move. Let us tell you a cautionary tale in which $125 million literally vanished into thin air. In 1999, NASA launched the Mars Climate Orbiter, a robotic craft intended to collect data on the red planet. On September 23, the craft disappeared. Did it self-destruct because of mechanical failure? Because of a design flaw? Stray meteorite? No. It turned out to be a simple error. NASA's scientists assumed that certain manufacturer's measurements had been metric. But they were wrong. As a result of this minor oversight, the craft went off course and is now permanently lost in space.

Years ago General Motors made a similar egg-in-the-face move, when it launched the Chevy Nova in Mexico—a well-priced car that they thought would appeal to families across the country. They got the engine purring beautifully, and made sure that every wheel was aligned. But they forgot one detail. They never bothered to check out what Nova means in Spanish. "No va" roughly translates as "no go." Ford committed a similar gaffe when it introduced the Pinto to Brazil; they discovered after the fact that the name means "tiny male genitals" in Portuguese.

It is important to ensure that the brand's DNA is replicated accurately throughout the commercial, presentation, or campaign. It's like a mirror. If you smash it into hundreds of pieces, you can still pick up a sliver and look back at your whole face. No matter how you slice up a Big Bang idea, each moment must re-create the entire gestalt of the brand, or the whole thing can fizzle.

With this in mind, we've written an entire instructional manual outlining the Big Bang concept behind Herbal Essences "Totally Organic Experience." Whether our commercial is shot in our New York office or in Singapore, the manual ensures that it will contain the Herbal DNA. Think of Sinatra, with his trademark hat, always tilted at a certain angle. He was his own walking, talking advertisement, and he never deviated from the brand he created in all the many decades he was at the top. That's why for so long he was regarded as the quintessential American pop singer.

At any point of contact with the consumer, you have to make sure you have maintained your Big Bang message, or you can lose your whole brand identity. Look what happened to Gap. In the 1980s, when it went from a homegrown store in San Francisco to an international phenomenon, Gap was synonymous with the classics: white cotton shirts, chinos, and jeans. However, in subsequent years, Gap lost the magic by becoming too fashion forward and losing its "we dress everyone in America" point of view. Speaking at a Goldman Sachs's retail conference in the fall of 2001, CEO Millard Drexler said, "We changed too much, too quickly, in ways that weren't consistent with our brands." After a disastrous 2001, when net earnings, which had peaked at $1,127,000 in 1999, dropped into the red, Drexler resigned. The stock price, from its historic high of over $50 a share, tanked to about $10 by winter 2001. Now, Gap has "jettisoned the high-fashion styles of recent years that drove away its traditional customers," according to the *Financial Times,* and is trying to rebuild that original DNA by relying on classics. Gap lost the magic not by a dramatic shift in strategy, veering off into selling other merchandise, but by altering ever so slightly the details of its original Big Bang idea.

You can't let one detail slide. Eric Lax, in *Woody Allen: A Biography*, points out that Allen works extremely hard at making sure every gesture is pure Woody. While it appears as though his routines are filled with impromptu moments, they aren't. "The pacing about, the flicking of the microphone cord, the seeming momentary forgetting of a line, the apparently spontaneous taking off of his glasses and rubbing his eyes while delivering a punch line, were all part of the act. He knew where he was and exactly what he was doing at every moment." While Allen might have used improvisation to come up with his material, he practiced and practiced until it was a precisely choreographed routine.

When we are producing a commercial, we go over and over it until we think every single moment is exactly on target. While our AFLAC duck might have a limited vocabulary, the way he says "AFLAC" is so nuanced that we had to hire two actors for his voice: The mild-mannered duck at the beginning of each commercial is the voice of Eric David, the art director who helped to create the duck. When the duck really gets his feathers ruffled, you hear the screechy voice of comedian Gilbert Gottfried.

Tom Ford, group creative director of Gucci, is another executive who realizes that every detail contributes to a brand's identity. Ford set an important strategy in place when he took the creative helm—to remake Gucci into a hot fashion brand. As a result, he orchestrated many changes in the company. But Ford also focuses on the minutiae of every moment. When Gucci is hosting an opening party for a new fragrance or product, Ford goes so far as to mark a little line on the volume dial of the stereo. He knows that the bass must be loud enough to pulse through every partygoer who walks in the door, yet soft enough so that she doesn't have to scream *"Did she get her eyes done?"* Every moment is orchestrated into a Gucci moment.

By taking to heart the fact that details are what make the Bang, and communicating that message through the company, missteps that could derail a Big Bang idea can be avoided. That doesn't mean you should take a deep breath and relax. On the contrary, it's much better to assume that disaster is lurking around every corner. . . .

ASSUME THE
Worst

Fear is a good thing. Fear, in fact, may well be the most powerful force in business. A couple of years ago, I remember reading a *New York Times* article about the entrepreneurial team behind Nantucket Nectars. It's a remarkable story—just eight years after selling peach juice out of a boat, college buddies Tom First and Tom Scott were running a company with $30 million in revenue. What kept them going? Fame and fortune, of course. But there was one other ingredient. Raw fear. "We still have nights where we don't sleep," First told the *Times*, "because we're still afraid of losing it all."

We have discovered that throughout the Big Bang process, a healthy dose of pessimism is the best antidote to obscurity. While you don't want to undermine the confidence of everyone around you, there's no more positive way to assure a Big Bang success than to accent the negative. Why?

Fear spurs creativity. Ironically, it is the only force strong enough to encourage people to take risks. Assuming the worst generates enough anxiety to motivate the troops to gamble on a controversial "out there" idea. When we're in the running for a new piece of business, I'm famous for saying to everyone working on the project, "We don't have it. It's not there." Of course, I've been in this business long enough to know that we *will* get it, but I want everyone to feel that it's up to them—and only them. The resulting low-grade panic inspires each person to assume that if she or he doesn't come up with an attention-grabber, every one of us may lose it all.

Fear is the primary weapon against roadblocks of all kinds. When a brand is doomed for extinction, for example, clients will go out on a limb to risk marketing ideas that have Big Bang promise. A case in point: If the Herbal Essences brand had been modestly healthy when we were asked to work on it, the client would have wanted to stick with the tried and true. As it happened, nothing could have been bleaker than the situation we faced. Everyone working on the project knew that we needed polarizing advertising to catapult the brand off hair care's Death Row.

Finally, fear is the only thing that keeps you from being a victim of your own success. Too many marketing professionals figure that once their Big Bang has exploded, their job is finished. We believe that the initial Bang is only the starting point. If you want that success to become permanent, you can never rest on your laurels. At KTG, we live in a state of mild terror, convinced that every Bang will turn into a fizzle. By assuming the worst, we have the courage to do the following.

Turn the Problem into the Solution

Traditionally, whenever marketing or advertising professionals start working with a new client, their first step is to identify the brand's top problem: No one can remember its name. It's the underdog. Consumers think it costs too much. Then they attempt to solve the problem by masking the issue or directing the consumer's attention elsewhere. In many cases, however, it's better to do the opposite and *highlight* the problem.

Target, for example, has long yearned for real estate in Manhattan. Their retailing model dictates that they need a big one-story space with parking, which in New York City is like finding a cab when it's pouring. Yet the company has the perfect reverse snob appeal that sells wildly to savvy New Yorkers. So what did they do? They suddenly stopped looking at the isle of Manhattan, and started looking at what was surrounding it: miles and miles of aisle-free water! And suddenly they hit upon the Big Bang idea: Build a store on a boat. It was only a temporary move—the ship docked at Pier 62 in Chelsea for two weeks before Christmas 2002—but the concept was a stroke of marketing genius. It became an overnight news story, with just about every paper and news outlet in the city covering the opening. People had to wait in line to get in. It was a grand marketing gesture that primed the pump for the moment Target does find space in Manhattan.

Manhattan itself is another example. The problem? It's an expensive place to do business. Yet New York City mayor Mike Bloomberg—recognizing that without corporate taxpayers, his job could get even worse—recently touted this very point at an economic conference at Rockefeller University. New York "is a high-

It's Good to Feel Bad

Never settle for an idea that doesn't scare you a little. When you're proposing to break all the rules, you should be on edge. At KTG we look for sweaty palms, irregular heartbeats, and the occasional outbreak of hives. Each of these symptoms may signal the emergence of a huge, Big Bang idea.

end product, maybe even a luxury product," he told the assembled corporate executives. Bloomberg turned the cost issue into a selling point. How do you know that New York is the best place in the world to do business? Because it's so expensive. You get what you pay for.

Just a few years ago, Tony Bennett's career was put back on track simply because his son decided to capitalize on the very thing that made Bennett an anathema to record companies: He's yesterday's hit.

By the late 1970s, Bennett's career hit a sour note. Lost to the hip-hop generation, Bennett could have bowed into graceful retirement, but there was one unfortunate black mark on this singer's dance card: Bennett was financially deep in the red. Over the years, his high life had landed him into terrible debt and the IRS was breathing down his neck. His son Danny decided to take the reins of Bennett's career.

Bennett Jr. decided to focus on the very fact that his father is the last of his breed. He's the only one left from the golden era of swing. The younger Bennett noticed that Bob Guccione Jr. was quoted in a local paper referring to Tony as "the essence of soul." Bennett Jr. called up Guccione and got him to publish an article on his father in Guccione's hip music magazine *Spin*. Not long after, Tony Bennett landed a part in the MTV Music Awards while his tribute album to Sinatra, *Perfectly Frank*, went gold. Tony Bennett's problem became the solution: He was from another era, which is why the younger generation couldn't get enough.

Many companies have turned a problem into a Big Bang.

Listerine, for example, has always been a bitter way to begin the day. But back in the 1970s, J. Walter Thompson, the ad agency for Listerine, got folks to gargle it up by making its awful taste a top selling point. "We were trying to see if we could stem the encroachment of Scope, which was about to go national," remembers Bernie Owett, a senior partner at J. Walter Thompson who ran the account. Up until that point, the euphemism for Listerine's taste was always "strong," Owett says. "At one point, that stopped work-ing, so we decided to hit it head-on and say it tastes bad." The burning flavor was proof that Listerine has the strength to kill off even the most offensive odors. The result? The mouthwash flew off the shelves with the famous line written by copywriter Nan Dillon, "The taste you'll hate. Twice a day." Owett claims that it was probably the most memorable Listerine campaign of the cen-tury.

Years ago, a Wal-Mart store manager in Louisiana had a prob-lem with shoplifting. The manager decided to post a "greeter," at the entrance to the store. The greeter, a friendly older gentleman, made thieves nervous and buyers feel welcome. "This odd experi-ment proved effective and eventually became standard practice across the company and a competitive advantage for Wal-Mart," say Collins and Porras in *Built to Last*. It also encapsulates Wal-Mart's message: We're the mom-and-pop superstore.

Recently, when we were asked to pitch Ruby Tuesday, we seized upon an issue that could have been perceived as a negative:

THE RAW QUALITY OF THE ADVERTISING SHOWS THAT THE ONLY THING RUBY TUESDAY KNOWS HOW TO COOK UP IS GOOD FOOD.

While the restaurant chain has been in existence for thirty years, they had never really done any advertising. Of course, what they did do was to pour all their money into operations. This fact inspired our creative team to come up with "not our first really good commercial." The ad depicts a spokesperson who launches into a spiel: "Since 1972 we at Ruby Tuesday have been trying to come up with a commercial as good as our food. So far no luck. We were close in '86. Because honestly we want our first commercial to be really, really good, and when we have that commercial we'll let you know . . . And no we don't have a slogan yet either." Our team turned the client's hesitation about advertising into an entire marketing campaign. CEO Sandy Beall loved it and bought the concept.

But no company has capitalized on its number-one problem more than Apple. The vast majority of computer users own PCs, which would make most competitors fall all over themselves listing the superior aspects of their product. Apple, instead, focuses on its underdog position. It all started in January 1984, when IBM was king, and Apple ran its famous 1984 commercial, and the company has never veered from this original marketing point: Only the select few use Macs. Their famous "Think Different" campaign, with its brilliant tagline, "Here's to the crazy ones," highlighted people like Picasso, Einstein, and Maria Callas. The point was simple: Don't let PC users tell you you're crazy for using a Mac, because it's the crazy ones that push the world forward.

Think Poor

When you're trying to come up ideas, think like a pauper, not like a king. Money often masks mediocrity. It can take any idea and masquerade it around as something big, bold, and beautiful. Then these overarched executions that never should have seen the light of day are allowed to hit the marketplace. And nothing dooms a product faster than misplaced hype. It creates an arrogant feeling about the brand, and makes customers suspicious and wary about ever trying your product again.

As Procter & Gamble's Rob Matteucci says, "You can throw money at advertising, but it's got to be memorable, provocative, distinctive stuff before it will cut through the clutter." He knows all too well. Ever heard of Physique shampoo? No? Well, that's the problem. Despite Proctor & Gamble's deep pockets, Matteucci says, very few people know that this product is available at the local

---

Perspiration Inspiration

When you're stuck for an idea, get out of the office at your first opportunity and get some exercise. First, you'll break the cycle of bad ideas clouding your thoughts. And, as everyone knows, exercise releases endorphins in the brain, bringing on a natural high that can put you in a creative frame of mind. In 1993, my husband and I were asked to write a song for an American Red Cross video to raise funds to provide services to refugees in Rwanda. Frustrated with my lack of inspiration, I went to the gym to clear my head. As I began to sweat out my worries on the StairMaster, I looked up to see news footage of the Rwandan refugees on CNN. The scenes brought me to tears. But the guy on the StairMaster next to me, after looking up at the TV, turned back to his magazine. His complete lack of empathy inspired an idea for a song entitled, "Don't Turn Away," to which Fred composed a heartfelt melody. Richie Havens performed the song with gut-wrenching emotion, and the video helped to raise millions for these starving refugees.

---

drugstore. "There was nothing about the introductory plan that was a Big Bang and we didn't wow anybody," he says. "It has taken us a long while to recover."

When we were presenting our "Totally Organic Experience" campaign to the folks at Clairol, my then colleague Douglas Atkin said to the client, "You've got ten million dollars and Pantene has eighty million dollars. If you do the same as Pantene, and simply talk about beautiful, lustrous hair, you might as well write a check to charity. You need to do something radical or don't bother." In fact, Nancy Crozier, director of marketing programs for The Nature Conservancy, points out that a Big Bang is the only option for a small budget: "In the nonprofit world, if you don't make a Big Bang, which ultimately has to influence behavior and thinking, your money is minimized. You don't have the luxury of trial and error." So no matter what your budget, ask yourself, What would I do if I had half the amount of money? Is the idea good enough to withstand limited funds? Will it break through, even if a consumer has only one exposure, be it on TV or in the stores?

Recently, BMW had a big success with some motorcycle ads by New York agency Merkley Newman Harty, despite the fact that their budget was very small. Up to this point, BMW bikes were bought by only a tiny percentage of motorcycle riders. Douglas Atkin, now the director of strategic planning at the agency, recalls that the planners working on the BMW account discovered two things: BMW riders were even more hard-core than Harley-Davidson riders, and everyone agreed that BMW makes the best bike. Yet the marketing at the time failed to address one important issue: The BMW symbol brought to mind BMW *car* drivers—hardly the unshaven, unkempt biker who rides from the tip of Alaska to the tip of Patagonia.

Figuring that bikers already know the bike is good, the creative team decided to buck conventional wisdom and focus almost exclusively on the rider. They came up with a series of grainy black-and-white images of rebellious guys under the open sky with taglines such as "If only the passing lane had a passing lane" and "Yeah, I have a hair stylist. His name's helmet." The spots were designed to speak to the rugged individuals with stained armpits and odometers that didn't rest. And speak they did: BMW's market share increased 30 percent just one year after the campaign debuted.

BMW could have done what many car companies are doing nowadays: Pay through the nose for the permission to play a rock hit by the Rolling Stones or Led Zeppelin, and shoot miles of footage lingering on the fast and snazzy vehicle. Instead, the modest budget forced the company to go with a disruptive way to get its message across, and it paid off in spades.

The marketing campaign behind Altoids is another example of small-budget genius. When the "curiously strong" mints were launched in the U.S. in 1995, the marketing campaign, by Leo Burnett USA, consisted of carefully targeted print ads and building-side murals. There were no TV spots. The ads, primarily one-liners such as "Luckily not available in extra strength" and "Our mints can beat up your mints," instantly caught on. The company engaged in inexpensive "guerrilla" marketing tricks, such as designing a tugboat in a New York harbor to look like an Altoids tin. Altoids eventually became the number-one breath freshener brand in stores, with market share of about 27 percent by January 2000. The ads won numerous awards and, according to *Crain's Chicago Business*, turned "a 200-year old English mint" into "an American icon."

Fall in Love with Plan B

All too often in the creative process, writers, directors, or clients set their heart on Plan A. Then a roadblock comes up. Most people grit their teeth and say, "By God, I made a plan and I'm going to stick with it!" or something else that Currency/Doubleday won't let us print. Then they look for a way to bulldoze through the problem, sometimes at great expense and often with mixed success. If, however, you are terrified that the entire project will vanish into thin air by dawn, you'll have the courage to abandon Plan A. Not only will you leave those roadblocks in the dust, but you'll often come up with something much better.

One day when Steven Spielberg was shooting *Raiders of the Lost Ark*, for example, Harrison Ford was slated to do a strenuous dueling scene. But, the story goes, Ford showed up to work with food poisoning. He told Spielberg that there was absolutely no way he could muster up the energy to do this fight scene, and really needed to take the day off. Desperate to keep the film on schedule, Spielberg begged Ford to stay, promising that he would find a way to get him off the set in one take. In a moment of utter panic, Spielberg and Ford came up with Plan B and let the camera roll.

Ford and his adversary eye each other, and the enemy suddenly draws his sword and brandishes it about like Errol Flynn on speed. With calculating precision, his opponent rushes toward Ford. At

KEEPING YOUR MESSAGE AFLOAT WHEN YOU DON'T HAVE A MEGA BUDGET.

the moment he is about to make shish kabob out of our hero, Ford, barely breaking a sweat, takes out his revolver and shoots the villain dead. This became one of the most talked-about scenes of the movie. Yet it never would have made it to celluloid if Plan A had worked out.

At KTG, we choose to see roadblocks as signposts. Perhaps Plan A wasn't meant to be. Perhaps a door shut for a reason. Perhaps something better is around the corner. After the World Trade Center attack, we canceled an AFLAC shoot that was supposed to take place in Venice, to avoid asking our staff to travel internationally at a time of great uncertainty. We were disappointed that we couldn't use a script that we all loved. But instead of trying to figure out a way to do the spot—shoot it in Toronto, against a Venetian-style backdrop?—we just abandoned the whole Venice concept.

Tom Amico and Eric David quickly got to work and created a new script, featuring Yogi Berra in a barbershop with the AFLAC duck. The finished spot ultimately became one of the most highly rated ads ever done for the insurance company, and last year the *Wall Street Journal* featured it as one of the ten best television commercials of the year. And in the end, we featured a true American icon at a time when it couldn't have been more appropriate.

I learned long ago to have a Plan B in my pocket whenever a presentation starts to crash and burn. When I was at Wells, Rich, Greene I wrote a funny Oil of Olay commercial, based on interviews with forty-year-old women who were sick to death of teenage models hawking products that they obviously didn't need. But I wasn't allowed to show it to the P&G client because I was warned that humor had no place in this incredibly serious category. Personally, I thought beauty care was a lot more of a yuck than health care and Medicare, but hey, what did I know? I was new to the category. We took other work to the meeting, but nothing seemed to spark any real enthusiasm from the Oil of Olay clients.

I started to realize that we were going to lose the client's interest altogether and soon became terrified that all our work would yield us bupkes. So I decided on the spot to go with Plan B. I took out my funny little script and sort of slipped it across to the client. The junior ankle-biters at Wells started nipping at me under the table.

But when the client read the ad, he immediately laughed out loud. It featured a forty-ish standup comedienne who blurted out to her audience, "If one more eighteen-year-old model sells me wrinkle cream, I'm going to scream!" P&G let us produce the spot, the talented Leslie Dektor agreed to shoot it, and it turned out to be a great ad for Oil of Olay.

Of course, when you abandon Plan A, that often means you have to coddle the person who came up with it. And that is no easy feat.

Stevie's Blind Spot

In the late 1980s, when art director Charlie Gennarelli and I were co-creative-directors on the Kodak account, along with executive account director Jerry Gottlieb, we received an interesting call. Stevie Wonder wanted to do a commercial for Kodak, and the company was just thrilled at the prospect. Now, most of the time working with celebrities is about as much fun as a colonoscopy. The preparation takes everything out of you, and just when you have nothing left to give, they stick it to you. But the idea of working with someone of Stevie Wonder's caliber was certainly exciting. The only problem was, Stevie wanted to be the spokesman for Kodak *film*. Clearly, a blind celebrity endorsing color photographs was not ideal. We needed to find a Plan B.

So it became our job to meet with Stevie Wonder, who was in Atlantic City at the time, and convince him to become a spokesman for Kodak batteries. But when I walked into the meeting, he immediately started talking about how happy he was to work with Kodak film.

"That's wonderful, Stevie," I told him, with perspiration dripping down my blouse, "but it's gonna be tricky having you talk about color and sharpness because, because—"

I just couldn't get the words out.

"Because I can't see?" Stevie said with a chuckle.

"Well, yeah," I mumbled.

Terrified that I'd lose his interest, and, in the end, this incredible opportunity for a celebrity endorsement, I mentioned as tactfully as I could that he'd be a more credible spokesman for Kodak batteries, since batteries are used for equipment like cassette players and electronic instruments.

He finally agreed to do a spot for the batteries.

By assuming the worst—that I could lose the whole business if I didn't bring Stevie Wonder on board—I was able to screw up the courage to convince this major celebrity to go with Plan B.

If It's Not Broke, Fix It Anyway

Success can be paralyzing. Once you've hit upon a great idea and your Big Bang is richocheting throughout the universe, you might be tempted to do nothing else. You've found a good formula, you figure, so stick with it. This may work in some fields, but in marketing, that kind of thinking is the HOV lane to failure. Too often companies want to put ideas on ice, thinking that they are preserving what's sacred, keeping the brand whole and virginal, when actually what they are doing is slowly making the brand or concept irrelevant and stale. The world is constantly moving, our lives are ever changing with every new CNN report, and there's no going back. We wake up to a slightly different planet every day of our lives.

At KTG we are never relaxed or comfortable with a great idea or campaign. Even the best Big Bang idea needs to be expanded and reinvented. You must be continually evolving or your consumer drifts elsewhere. If a campaign doesn't change, it becomes like an oil painting on the living room wall: No one even sees it anymore.

It is success, in fact, that should create the pressure to keep evolving: Now that you've got the consumer's attention, don't lose it. Ask yourself, "What if the worst happened tomorrow?" When British publisher Bloomsbury, which came out with the first *Harry Potter* book, realized what a huge hit it was, chief executive Nigel Newton immediately started planning for life after Harry, planting the seeds for further penetration into the U.S. market. As Martin Nuechtern, Procter & Gamble's president of global hair care, puts it, we must have the ability "to understand the core idea behind a great idea and then take it elsewhere."

Just the act of creating a Big Bang can put your brand in a precarious, albeit successful, state. By definition, a Big Bang disrupts the norm and creates a new universe. But this universe can quickly become inhabited with competitors. Once we created the "Totally Organic Experience" campaign for Herbal Essences, imitators started popping up everywhere, selling their products with sensual and experiential promises. More important, a universe that seems revolutionary and paradigm-shifting one minute, seems old and hackneyed the next. In fact, it could be said that the more attention you get, the quicker your revolutionary idea can wear out in the marketplace. Thus you need to disrupt the very universe you created.

At KTG, despite our success with AFLAC, we are always fearful that it could all end tomorrow. Every commercial we make has to disrupt the universe created by the previous one. The second commercial took the duck out of his natural habitat—a city park—and put him in a steam room. We then incorporated celebrities to upstage the duck. We eventually allowed a human being to say the word "AFLAC." We just finished filming a commercial with comedian Chevy Chase. One of our latest spots takes place in a tacky Las Vegas wedding chapel, and the duck is not even there. Instead of quacking "*AFLAC!*" to oblivious onlookers, he's clear across town, tapping his webbed foot at a Wayne Newton concert. This constant expansion is the only way to keep the campaign surprising.

Likewise, the Toys "R" Us song has been rewritten a zillion different ways—as a rock song, a ballad, a jazz riff. Several years ago we tracked down the child actors from the original blockbuster Toys "R" Us commercial, dressed them up in the same clothes, and reenacted the entire spot, juxtaposing old footage of them as kids with their current adult selves.

This forced evolution is the only way to keep a Big Bang marketing idea in perpetual motion. The story of M&Ms proves our point. We all remember the cute little animated characters in the sixties and seventies who "melt in your mouth, not in your hands." These little candy characters became overnight celebrities and helped to make M&Ms a top-selling sweet. But the M&M manufacturer, Mars, knows their hard-won market share could melt away faster than a candy bar left out in the sun. Every few years the company introduces a new innovation, including mini M&Ms, almond M&Ms, peanut-butter M&Ms, and seasonal colors for Christmas and Easter.

All this change has paid off: They have been into space with NASA's astronauts, and can count both presidents Reagan and Clinton as fans. When the company asked the public to vote on which new color the company should use (blue, pink, or purple), nearly 10 million votes were cast (blue won).

Just a few years ago Mars brought back its animated "spokescandies." But this time, they are not the cutesy, sweet M&Ms of a more innocent era. Recognizing that their old characters are dated, the company created totally twenty-first-century candies, with attitude and smart comeback lines. "Green," the first "female" M&M spokescandy, who debuted with the tagline, "I Melt for No One," sparred during a Super Bowl game with Dennis Miller about the sexual potency of green-colored M&Ms.

The trick is to know what you can change—and what you can't. There are some unchangable equities that can never be tampered with. We will always use a Pekin species of duck for AFLAC. Classic Coke's logo is red and white—even if it's drastically different from the original. Burberry's classic check will never disappear—though it's now showing up on watchbands, diaper bags, and thong sandals. Tiffany, while they may sell you Elsa Peretti's latest, will always wrap it in a blue box. According to brand expert Randi Dorman, "The reason brands exist is so that consumers can

215

be promised a certain kind of experience. A certain amount of trust and familiarity is built over the years. You don't want to change just for change's sake, but you want to maintain relevance to your target."

Dorman cites Crest's recent redesign as an example. Crest is an old, venerated brand, but its former white packaging with red and blue letters was outdated. This healthy, pharmaceutical look was "relevant to the consumer fifteen, twenty years ago when toothpaste was all about health and dentists," Dorman says, "but the consumer has shifted. Whitening products started to come out, and the consumer perception is now that if your teeth are whiter they are cleaner, and therefore healthier." Crest turned to Interbrand to redesign its packages. "They had to balance the trust and heritage of the brand with the idea that Crest is innovative and could help to transform your smile," explains Dorman.

Interbrand's new design kept the same typeface for the logo, and didn't alter the red color for the letter "C," which is a solid marker for the brand. But they changed many other aspects of the packaging, including turning the background a rich blue with a starburst. The end result "created a fresh new look, but still maintained the Crest identity," says Dorman. After the launch of the redesign, Crest, which had lost its number-one position to Colgate, once again became the top-selling brand.

Perhaps the best illustration of balancing brand identity and relevance is the "A Diamond Is Forever" campaign, written in 1947 for the Diamond Trading Company (then known as De Beers). While the tagline never changed, the ads kept up with the times. The first ads depicted World War II veterans coming home and presenting diamond rings to faithful fiancées. Through the seventies and eighties, competing against a rising tide of luxury products, the spots starred everyone from hippies to conspicuous consumers. Then came the "Shadows" commercials, which didn't even show people. The ads were simply silhouettes of typical "diamond" moments such as a proposal or a wedding anniversary. The campaign has earned billions for the diamond industry, and was chosen as one of the top ten campaigns of the twentieth century by *Advertising Age.*

Assuming the worst means you need to see the glass empty throughout the Big Bang process. When it comes to people, however, you should always see the glass half full. . . .

A MARKETING IDEA CAN LIVE FOREVER WHEN IT CONTINUALLY DAZZLES
CONSUMERS WITH TIMELESS MESSAGES.

Create

A FERTILE UNIVERSE

We often look back at the explosive growth of our company and try to picture what it would have been like if any of the people we have hadn't come to KTG. And it is almost unimaginable. It would be like trying to imagine what would have happened to the universe if, in the original Big Bang, every particle had not consented to play its part. Because every writer, every graphic designer, every assistant, every account person at our company has been, in part, responsible for moving us forward at explosive speed, for making our business go "*bang!*" Minus just one individual, we would have had a different company, albeit one probably not quite so successful or so rich in spirit and soul.

When you realize that *every single member* of your organization is critical, possessing the ability to make powerful contributions to the creative process, you begin to see that everyone you work with plays a part in driving the company forward. It is your job to discover how to arrange and use them all to suit the task at hand, like a conductor directing an orchestra. Since employees' personalities are as diverse as their talents, choreographing this orchestration is an art form in itself.

Yet it's probably the single most important part of the Big Bang process. Creating a fertile universe for your staff is the only way to ensure future creative and financial success. Big Bangs won't happen unless your employees are continually prodded into a positive frame of mind. At KTG, we accomplish this by ignoring several dictates of traditional business etiquette.

Bring Your Baggage to Work

Most executives are trained to draw a line in the sand between the personal and professional. Don't bring your problems to the office, don't take business too much to heart, and above all don't have lengthy discussions of private issues at work. But if you ask people to check their personal lives at the door, they are not really bringing their whole emotional selves to the job. They are merely bringing a polished veneer of themselves, with no depth or character. If you think of people as onions, each of us buried under layers and layers of "socialized" skins, then you realize that it's only by peeling away the layers that you can discover something meaningful and true. So we deliberately buck the norm. We encourage people to bring their whole being to work, warts and all. Although we sometimes know more than we care to about someone's late credit card payment, most people feel more accepted here than in previous jobs. By breaking down the wall between business and personal, we can freely climb into each other's emotional core.

For example, after 9/11, all of us were edgy, anxious, and depressed. The World Trade Center was only a couple of miles away from our office, and employees hurriedly leaving our Midtown location could see the plumes of smoke from the burning buildings, and later see them suddenly collapse as they looked down Fifth Avenue. In the weeks that followed, we found work almost impossible. Afraid to air their feelings, people retreated to the stream of apocalyptic CNN reports flashing from their laptops. Finally, I called the KTG staff together and announced that during group idea sessions it would be totally acceptable for people to interrupt the meeting with a detailed account of their nightmares, their anxieties, or a healthy flow of tears. By bringing our personal feelings back into the workplace, we were able, as a group, to stumble back into creating, trying to move forward, just as people did throughout the city and across the country.

Be Manipulative

Why shaping actions or events—being manipulative—has been given such a negative rap is beyond us. Of course, we would never advocate manipulating a person in a way that undermines, ridicules, or financially hurts him or her. But when you influence an outcome, a staffer, or a meeting to reach a positive conclusion, then everyone profits. In fact, without some form of manipulation of the world around us, we could never create a Big Bang factory.

Managers can influence the environment around them simply by the impressions they leave on everyone they work with. As Geshe Michael Roach writes in his Buddhist philosophical book

Hire in Sixty Seconds

We can usually tell within 60 seconds of meeting someone whether they are right for the job or not. In marketing, an Ivy League diploma is impressive, but passion, street smarts, and intelligence count more. We've never hired someone who doesn't immediately get our jokes. Likable people aren't just fun to work with; they tend to work better in groups and make better employees.

The Diamond Cutter, "things occur to us in exact accord with how we treat those around us." It is our belief that if those impressions are positive, they will positively affect the actions and attitudes of the whole company, and everyone associated with it. In the best-selling book *First, Break All the Rules: What the World's Greatest Managers Do Differently*, Gallup researchers Marcus Buckingham and Curt Coffman revealed the results of a study of employees of the BestBuy electronics store chain: In the most productive Best-Buy store, nearly half the employees felt that managers nurtured and listened to them, creating an environment where the employees felt valued and respected. In the least productive store, only 11 percent of all the employees felt that way. Were those in the productive store manipulated by their bosses? You betcha.

On the other hand, one disrespectful or thoughtless remark can undermine relationships that have taken a lot of effort to establish, and profoundly deflate the entire creative process, paralyzing the free flow of ideas. This "deflation" has a physiological effect on employee performance as well as a psychological one, as Jim Loehr and Tony Schwartz note in a recent issue of the *Harvard Business Review*. "Just as positive emotions ignite the energy that drives high performance, negative emotions—frustration, impatience, anger, fear, resentment, and sadness—drain energy. Over time, these feelings can be literally toxic, elevating heart rate and blood pressure, increasing muscle tension, constricting vision, and ultimately crippling performance."

So we work hard to create positive impressions. That means the assistant, the CEO, and the mail carrier are all treated with the same respect and courtesy. We strive to answer every phone message and résumé letter, and virtually every supplier gets an appreciative call back—even if that company did not win a bid on a production. We can't tell you how many thankful letters and emails we have gotten in return, or how many times it has eventually led to us winning a new piece of business. The universe of marketing and advertising is ultimately very small, and politeness is a rare commodity—so it is remembered. But it is the manager who must set the tone: People do as you do, not as you say.

Of course, we're not the first company that has discovered that maintaining a positive environment is a good way to manipulate people to produce the way you want them to. The Container Store, a storage and organization business, is a great example of a company that attempts to treat its employees and customers with courtesy and respect. The company invests a lot of time and energy in teaching new hires, giving them some 235 hours of training (the industry standard is roughly 7 hours). Its vendors are never neglected: As cofounder Garrett Boone said in a recent interview with *Fast Company* magazine, "The only way that we can come into the housewares world and duke it out with the Wal-Marts is to have much better relationships with our vendors than those other mass merchants do." The result? First, the Container Store has been listed as one of *Fortune* magazine's 100 Best Companies to Work For three years in a row. Moreover, all of this good will has paid off. The company has seen 20 percent or higher annual sales growth for several years running. It makes sense to us.

Be a "Yes" Person

Too often, the minute someone has the title "executive" laser-printed on his business card, he assumes it's his job to say "No" as emphatically and often as possible. But the ability to say only "no" is the sign of a very limited vocabulary. "No" is the coward's way out. "No" doesn't commit you to having a risky idea. "No" doesn't enlighten or instruct. It doesn't move things forward. It simply shuts the process down.

A much more constructive word is "yes." Perhaps women are more predisposed to find ways to say "yes" in situations where others might say "no." Why? Maybe it's because so many of us are mothers and have had to face down a toddler who demands to wear shorts in winter. Mothers know you can't say, "No, you can't, it's

10 degrees outside!" Such a response will only aggravate the situation. Instead we deflect, while still trying to respect the child's feelings, "Yes, what a great idea! Why don't you wear your shorts now, and then, when we go outside, we'll put on those nice blue jeans! Blue is my favorite color, is it yours?"

"Yes," in our experience, is the best way to way to create business bonanzas. We don't know why more people don't realize that the validation of someone's feelings and opinions can help to open the floodgates of collaborative relationships and creative thinking. Too many people worry that if they say "yes" to a colleague's idea, they diminish the value of their own point of view. But recognizing and acknowledging someone else's good idea doesn't make a win-lose situation. Often the team effort can make it a win-win for both of you.

But what about when the idea or suggestion isn't a viable one? When a client comes up with an idea that I think is unworkable, I usually respond with a comment like, "I'm going to write that down," or "I'll give that some thought and get back to you." The result is the same—the idea dies a peaceful death moments after it's

Prod with a Nod

At our brainstorming meetings, in order to encourage the discussion of ideas and discourage internal reveries, we encourage direct eye contact with the speaker and lots of supportive nodding and smiling, even with only half-baked ideas. We call it "prodding by nodding." It helps to draw out the speaker, and lead all of us to discuss what could very well become a Big Bang campaign.

aired—but I find that egos stay intact and each person feels respected.

When a creative team comes in with an idea lacking in explosive potential, we could easily tell them they just don't have it, and dismiss them. What would follow is a lot of self-doubt from the team, fretting whether they will ever get it, and whether they have what it takes to find it in the first place. This just creates a whirlwind of negative energy, and hinders the kind of optimism and energy that can lead to a Big Bang idea.

Instead we tell them that they have an explosive, attention-grabbing concept in them somewhere, beneath their conconsciousness, waiting to be found. They just need to explore more ways to tap into that subconscious energy. This makes the Big Bang exploration a finite process, rather than one that is never-ending and possibly futile.

Nonetheless, we believe that settling for a "little bang" or a "good enough" idea is not an option. Massaging a "good" idea in the hope that it will be magically transformed into greatness virtually never works, and can curtail a team from continuing the hunt and discovering something truly novel and explosive. This can rob everyone, the client and the creative team, from having a Big Bang. So we try to inspire our staff to let go of the mediocre idea and reach for a genuinely explosive concept.

This ability to deflect and parry can be a useful negotiating skill. A few years back we had a budget negotiation with a client who wanted to spend a few hundred thousand dollars on a campaign that required a much larger budget in order to become a Big Bang. Rather than tell them that this was an unrealistically low budget, and ask them point blank if they could spend more money—knowing full well they'd just say no—I drew them out in a conversation that ran something like the following:

Linda: "What's your budget?"

Client: "Six hundred thousand dollars."

"OK. And you would go as high as?"

"Maybe $750 thousand."

"And if you were going for an A director, for just one of those spots, how much would you go for?"

"OK, a million."

"And if you want to do all the spots with an A director, you'd go as far as—"

"Well, maybe, $1.2 million."

"If it meant that you might lose the director you want because of the fee, what would your ceiling be?"

"The top would be 2 million."

Of course, I could have taken them at their word at the outset, and tried to work within the smaller budget. But I would have found myself compromising what we could deliver. I realized their first response might not have accurately reflected their real position, and I knew they would regret scaling back on the ad campaign later. So I deflected and parried until I had a more accurate budget.

And the commercials were awesome.

Throw Your Ideas Away

"You can accomplish anything in life," Harry S. Truman once said, "provided that you do not mind who gets the credit." One of the hardest things for many of us to do is to share the glory. Whenever we have a great idea, it's tempting to want to claim the credit and bask in the adulation. But at KTG we believe that letting others share ownership of an idea increases the odds of it becoming a Big Bang. "It's like a relationship," says Paul Zuckerman. "Not everyone does equal work, but together we do great stuff. A plus B plus C equals Q. This would never happen with just one person. You need a group." Talented people tend to be competitive and territorial, but the only way to enjoy sustained success is with group effort.

In *The Evolution of Cooperation,* political scientist Robert Axel-

> **Hire Doers**
>
> Too many marketers spend endless time preparing slides, crafting colored bar graphs, and churning out regurgitations of data analysis rather than solving problems. It's like trying to fix a radio by theorizing for days about why it's not working, when you can just open it up and realize it needs two new AA batteries. That's why we hire doers rather than theorists, workers rather than supervisors. People who *do* do, people who talk about doing, inevitably, *don't*.

rod used mathematical models to explain human actions. He ran computer programs that played a version of the Prisoner's Dilemma, a classic social science exercise where two prisoners are being interrogated separately. If prisoner A rats the other guy out, he goes free, and prisoner B goes to jail for a decade—and vice versa. If both stay mum, however, both get only one year of jail time. The most "cooperative" computer program won the game, leading Axelrod to postulate that cooperation creates long-term stability. Recently, researchers at Emory University in Atlanta, using a version of the Prisoner's Dilemma experiment, found that cooperating with others actually induces a physical high akin to that created by pictures of pretty faces, money, and desserts. (Although the last time I had a slice of chocolate cheesecake, I wouldn't have shared it with a living soul.)

When a great idea is born at KTG, everybody in the company feels like they've nurtured and helped to hatch it. Indeed, one of the reasons why we have so many people work on each project is so that everyone will reap the benefits of the success. This creates an exhilarating "high" that the entire group wants to achieve again and again.

Gordon Bethune, the chairman and CEO of Continental Airlines, uses a similar philosophy. Rather than offering just praise and a proverbial pat on the back to his employees, he puts his money where his mouth is. In the 1990s, the airline was notorious for its poor on-time performance. Bethune decided to authorize the company to give every employee below the director level one hundred dollars for every month that the airline achieved first place in the Department of Transportation's on-time ranking. He gave sixty-five dollars per month for every month the airline was in second or third place. "We quickly went from the tenth on-time airline to the first," says Bethune's marketing chief, Bonnie Reitz. "For the last five years, we have been the number-one on-time airline period."

Managers of the international restaurant chain Ruby Tuesday are invited several times a year to an all-expenses-paid trip to the company's Ruby Tuesday Lodge, a luxurious four-star inn, according to CEO Sandy Beall. "This is unheard of in our business," says Beall, "but it keeps great employees energized and passionate enough about their jobs that they don't leave. And if you don't have the right people in place," Beall continues, "you'll always be second rate." Beall clearly has no compunctions about throwing the credit for his chain's unbelievable success right back to the employees themselves.

Great managers never do. In fact, through our many encounters with CEOs of very successful companies, we have noticed one similarity: The word "I" seems to be missing from their vocabulary.

Act as If Your Life Depends on It

Twenty-three years ago, with nothing but a weak résumé and a handful of stick-figure ads, I made a series of cold calls to every advertising person I could rustle up among my friends and acquaintances. Very few people bothered to call me back. But one who did was Bernie Owett, the former co-executive creative director and senior partner of J. Walter Thompson. Despite the fact that

I had no advertising experience, he told me he would be happy to see me. I was thrilled. Three weeks later I arrived at a swank Lexington Avenue office building, and was met by Owett, who rushed me into his spacious tweed-fabric-walled office on the twelfth floor. I showed Owett the flimsy little spec book that creative director Manning Rubin, a business associate of my father's, had helped me piece together. It was filled with a corny Cracker Jack jingle, lots of bad shampoo ads, and an idea for Dunkin' Donut "holes," an invention of mine that, alas, was too early for its time ("Munchkins" didn't come out until much later).

I was nervous as hell and not just because my marketing knowledge could fit into a thimble. *I had no idea where I was!* In my exuberance to be granted an interview, I had written down Bernie's name, his title, and his office address, but I had neglected to jot down the name of the advertising company he worked for. I frantically searched the kazillion awards that adorned his office, hoping that one contained the name of the company that employed him. No such luck. Nonetheless, I somehow stumbled my way through the interview process; I must have said something witty or remarkable, because the next thing I know he's on the phone recommending me for a junior copywriter job.

The impression Bernie Owett made on me that day led me to the way we run our business at KTG. I went on to work for Owett, and never saw him be nasty or raise his voice. He was always a true gentleman, illustrating to me the importance of acting decently and doing the right thing. I've tried to carry that ethic with me for over twenty-five years.

You never know when the impressions you make on others will come back full circle. A year ago, out of the blue, I received a call from a woman named Joanne Miserandino, who worked at one of our sister agencies overseas. She mentioned that she would be in the U.S. the following week and would love to meet with us. I assumed she was looking to network with other New York agencies of Publicis, our mutual parent company. Although we were in the middle of several new business pitches, we were happy to meet with her, and offer whatever assistance she needed. When we finally met, she looked quite familiar, although I could not accurately place where I knew her from.

Little did I know then that this conversation would lead to landing one of our biggest accounts.

It turned out that Miserandino was a managing account director on Procter & Gamble's global Dawn and Swiffer accounts, and the company was looking to find an agency within the Publicis network to partner with in New York. Having several options, I was flattered, yet surprised, that she would recommend KTG. After all, living in Europe for the past twenty years, how much could she know about our work or our resources? Containing my curiosity no longer, I finally blurted out, "It's great that you called me, but I'm still wondering, why us?"

She just smiled and said, "Twenty-two years ago, I was a junior account executive on the Kodak account and you were the creative director. Even though I was the lowest hire on the food chain, you always treated me with respect. I never forgot that. And that's why I'm hoping to bring the business here." In the end, she recommended us to her client and her bosses and we ended up with two hefty new accounts that will soon be the recipients of some Big Bang campaigns.

Not Everyone Wants a Bang for Their Buck

No matter how hard you try, or how many arms you twist, you can't have a truly explosive marketing or advertising plan if your client or boss doesn't want one. This seems obvious, of course, but often our egos cannot accept the reality that none of us can fly solo. At the end of the day, it's usually someone else's money that's invested, and it takes two to go Bang.

Of course, with all our successes over the years, it's always difficult to come to terms with the fact that some companies shy away from embracing the concept of a Big Bang. Some companies are too afraid to take the leap into what is often seen as risky territory. Last year we pitched a financial company that had a virtually invisible presence in the marketplace, yet had a client list that included over 80 percent of the Fortune 1000 companies in America. This amazing fact prompted us to present a tongue-in-cheek commercial that substituted every brand name on the screen—whether it was a car, a beer, or a handbag—with theirs. This "Name Behind the Name" campaign really hit home the fact that although they had a low profile, they were part of the financial acumen behind the success of so many iconic brands.

Yet the CEO, though he was amused by the campaign, didn't feel that his company deserved the bravado it promised. *Hello?* Can *anyone* afford to be shy in this cluttered market? Imagine if the CEO of Intel had said, when presented with the "Intel inside" campaign, "We're just a piece of hardware in a computer. We're not so important!" If you're not your own feistiest advocate, who else will be?

Still, there is an art to knowing when gentle persuasion turns into coercion. Usually we are very good at stepping back and saying, "OK, maybe next time." But we had one experience where we just refused to read the room and rely on our feminine intuition.

Robin and I had flown out to meet the representative of a company whose business we were just dying to represent. We had heard that this client was rather conservative, but we were sure that once they saw what we had, they would sign on with us. However, we knew we were in trouble when, after showing our agency reel, we heard not a single sigh or giggle. Next, we launched headlong into our Big Bang philosophy. But it was like presenting to an oil painting—everyone was motionless. Robin and I slogged on, determined to make this client understand just how much a Big Bang would help the company. We continued digging ourselves in deeper and deeper with every case study we threw up on Power-Point. Finally, after what seemed like an eternity of silence, our prospective client deigned to speak to us: "You know, I've worked on a lot of businesses and you might say hair care or insurance is complicated, but I can tell you that the custom furniture business is something you can work on for years and years and never really understand."

"Really," Robin was tempted to retort. "I don't think it's all that hard. You sell cabinets. Most people know how to use one of those. You open the door, you put your dishes in, and then you close it!" Needless to say, we didn't get the account.

After the fact, we were relieved. Our philosophy and way of working isn't for everyone, and not everyone is ready to take the leap into creating a disruptive Big Bang campaign.

Make It Personal

One truly great by-product of working at a company focused on creating Big Bangs is that this way of thinking inevitably spills into your personal life. And sometimes in the most unlikely of ways.

Thirteen years ago I was diagnosed with breast cancer, and although I was eventually told that my disease was considered "cured," my surgeon had advised me not to have children. Refusing to take "no" for an answer, I decided, after many previously unsuccessful attempts at pregnancy, to make an appointment with Dr. Larry Norton, one of the world's leading breast cancer oncologists, to ask his advice.

After my examination, I sat in Dr. Norton's office at the Memorial Sloane-Kettering Cancer Center and waited for his verdict. He told me, "You are cured. Go ahead and get pregnant." Barely able to contain my joy, I said, "How can I thank you?" He responded warmly, with the smile of someone not accustomed to relaying good news, "Just send me a picture of the baby."

After two years of trying, I did get pregnant, and went on to have a beautiful baby boy, Michael. Three years later, we were blessed again with our lovely daughter, Emily. I wanted to send Dr. Norton a picture of them both, but I held back, knowing in my gut that someday I would discover a way to express my gratitude. Six years later, I finally got my chance to deliver a Big Bang thank-you.

I was invited to a breakfast honoring Dr. Norton, sponsored by the Women's Executive Circle of the United Jewish Communities. Throughout the event I could barely contain my excitement. After an inspiring lecture, Dr. Norton opened the floor for questions. Determined to be the first to speak, I shot my hand in the air and stood up.

"Dr. Norton," I said, "I doubt that you will remember me. But ten years ago I was diagnosed with breast cancer, and after my surgery, despite the advice of my surgeon, you told me that it would be safe to get pregnant. Your advice meant more than anything in the world to me at the time. I asked if there was any way I could thank you. You simply said, 'Just send me a picture of the baby.' "

With a faint hint of recollection in his eyes, Dr. Norton chimed in, "So show me the picture!"

"Not only do I have one picture, I have two," I told him. "Our daughter Emily is now six years old, and our son Michael is nine. Michael began playing chess at age four, and just one year later he won the United States Kindergarten Chess championship. He's now one of the top children's chess players in the world; he has just returned from Spain, where he competed in the annual world youth chess championships. A couple of years ago a book was written about my son's accomplishments. Before Michael left for school this morning I told him about you, and how much of a difference you have made in our lives. So Michael thought you might want a copy of his book, and he autographed it just for you."

Silence blanketed the room. Dr. Norton, with a catch in his throat, said, "This is one of the greatest gifts I've ever received; it's the reason that I do what I do." The room erupted into applause, and I could barely catch my breath. I had waited for years to thank this man. Now the memory of this event would last a lifetime.

Then, suddenly, out of the sea of tears and smiles that swept over the group, a woman next to me leaned over and whispered, "Now *that's* a Kodak moment."

THIS BOOK WOULD HAVE
BEEN LONGER, BUT WE DIDN'T
WANT TO GO INTO

CHAPTER
11

WE'RE SURE YOU UNDERSTAND.

INDEX